NINJA FOODI 2-BASKET AIR FRYER COOKBOOK FOR BEGINNERS

EASY AIR FRYER RECIPES WITH STEP BY STEP INSTRUCTIONS TO FRY, GRILL, ROAST, BAKE AND DEHYDRATE

MARILENA TRENTINO

TABLE OF CONTENTS

INTRODUCTION

Hello and Welcome!

The ninja foodi 2-baskets air fryer is a new kitchen appliance amongst the wide range of air fryers. The best thing about this appliance is that it has two baskets. You can cook two different foods at the same time with two different or same settings.

If you are busy and have no time for cooking delicious and healthy food, then this appliance is best for you because it saves your time and cooks yummy and healthy food. Ninja foodi 2-baskets have many functions. You can prepare restaurant-style meals in your kitchen with the help of this appliance. It fulfills your cooking needs. It has super "dual zone" technology that allows the appliance to be put on either single cook mode or multi cook mode. The single cook mode works when you are using a single basket. With dual cook mode, you can cook something food in two baskets or different food in two baskets.

With this appliance, you can air fryer, bake, the air crisp, broil, dehydrate, and more. You can press mode according to food. If you want to bake, and then press "bake" mode or if you're going to air fry, then press "air fryer" mode.

My cookbook "ninja foodi 2-baskets air fryer with dual zone technology" has 70 yummy recipes. Take advantage of any recipes provided in my cookbook to enjoy the meal that keeps your health maintained.

I divided recipes into different chapters such as breakfast, chicken and poultry recipes, beef, lamb, and pork recipes, seafood and fish recipes, and vegetable recipes. All recipes are tasty and healthy.

The ninja foodi 2-baskets air fryer is easily available at an affordable price. You can buy it at local stores or online. According to recipe instructions, you can adjust temperature and cooking time onto ninja foodi air fryer and prepare tasty food. Now, stop sacrificing the taste and enjoy a yummy meal using this appliance. The ninja foodi 2-baskets air fryer has a 40 to 240 degrees c range of temperature.

QUICK COOK, EAT TASTY!

HOW TO USE THE NINJA FOODI 2-BASKET AIR FRYER

If you want to use Ninja foodi 2-basket air fryer, you should know about all functions. It is not complicated to use. You can use it simply after reading this book.

Step: 1
• Prepare your food like rolls, sandwiches, or others. Divide your food into two different baskets.

Step: 2
• Return basket into Ninja foodi 2-baskets air fryer.

Step: 3
• A select method such as "air fryer" mode for Zone 1 with "recipe calls" temperature and "recipe calls" cooking time.

Step: 4
• Press the "MATCH COOK" button to copy the setting for Zone 2.

Step: 5
• Press the "START/PAUSE" button to initiate the cooking.

Step: 6
• If you want to flip the food, open the lid, flip over the food, and cook according to recipe cooking time.

Step: 7
• When done, remove it from the appliance and transfer it to the serving plate.

• Serve and enjoy your food with your family.

All cooking modes are pretty simple. No one is complicated. You should follow these simple steps and prepare your food.

TIPS TO USE THE NINJA FOODI 2 BASKET AIR FRYER

The following tips with enhancing your cooking experience with Ninja foodi 2-basket air fryer.

- When using the Dual Zone technology, either with the Smart Cook or Match Cook settings, the user manual recommends adding anywhere from 3 to ten more minutes of air-frying time, as the appliance's energy is divided within the two cooking Zones.
- You can start and pause the cooking in both baskets or individually, allowing you to shake the baskets or toss the food being air-fried, roasted, reheated or dehydrated to guarantee an even cooking. Shaking and tossing often is encouraged for even results.
- Both baskets come equipped with an optional Crisper Plate that can easily be attached depending on the food item. Using the Crisper Plates is recommended when air frying and when roasting food cut in smaller pieces.
- The average cooking temperature for most foods is 390°F (200°C), and the average cooking time ranges from 10 to 20 minutes. Add more minutes if using the Dual-Zone Technology. Dehydration takes place at 135°F (60°C) for fruit and vegetables, and 150°F (65°C) for meat. Dehydrating requires an average of between 6-8 hours.
- You can wash baskets and crisper plates in the dishwasher or by hand. Clean the central unit and control panel with a damp cloth.

The Smart Finish and Match Cook Dual-Zone Technologies

What makes the Ninja Foodi 2 Basket Air Fryer unique are its two baskets, each 8 x 6.5 inches in dimension, and a capacity of around five hundred grams. The baskets work independently and can air-fry, roast, reheat and dehydrate different foods simultaneously, even at different temperature and time settings.

- **Smart Finish.** The Smart Finish setting allows you to cook two foods at the same time, each in its own basket governed by a Zone. You can cook different foods despite differences in setting, time and temperature. The Smart Finish Technology programs the air-frying times in both Zones to ensure the two baskets finish at the same time. If Zone 1 is programmed for a cooking time longer than the timer set for Zone 2, Zone 1 will begin air frying, and Zone 2 will catch up, ensuring both Zones finish cooking simultaneously.

- **Match Cook.** The Match Cook setting allows you to copy the cooking setting, time and temperature from one Zone to the other. This allows you to cook two batches of the same food or two different foods that require the same cooking time, setting and temperature.

FUNCTIONS OF NINJA FOODI 2 BASKET AIR FRYER

Air Frying Settings

The Ninja Foodi 2 Basket Air Fryer does more than air frying food to crispy perfection; it has several cooking modes that automatically adjust the temperature and airflow in each Zone individually for the best results.

- **Air-Fry.** Air-frying is the Ninja Foodi 2 Basket Air Fryer primary function. Intense streams of hot air air-fry the food to achieve crispy and golden results. This mode is ideal for chips, fries, breaded meat and other food that would benefit from deep frying.

- **Roast**. Rather than cooking food to crispness, the Ninja Foodi 2 Basket Air Fryer Roast mode allows you to cook tender meat and vegetables with steady temperatures for fork-tender results. Not dissimilar to a convection oven, roasting food gives the Dual Zone air fryer versatility.

- **Reheat**. A gentler setting that allows you to reheat cooked food without burning or drying it. This setting is ideal for reheating leftovers and food cooked ahead of time. The heat intensity is enough to reheat food evenly. This setting is also suitable for warming bread and other food that benefits from being served warm.

- **Dehydrate**. The Dehydrate setting in the Ninja Foodi 2 Basket Air Fryer is a unique mode that allows you to dehydrate fruit, vegetables and meat at constant, low temperatures for extended periods of several hours. The Dual-Zone Technology will enable you to dehydrate different items in distinct settings in each basket.

MAINTAIN AND CLEANING THE APPLIANCE

Maintain and clean up the Ninja foodi air fryer is pretty simple. Follow these simple steps:

• Firstly, unplug the appliance before start cleaning. Let it cool if it is hot. Then, start cleaning.

• After that, remove both air fryer baskets from the appliance. Keep them aside.

• When cooled, remove the plates and wash them thoroughly.

• Use soapy water and wash the air fryer baskets. But keep in mind; avoid using hard scrubber because it will damage the surface.

• Use soft scrub to clean the food stuck.

• Clean the main unit with a piece of cloth.

• When everything is cleaned, let them dry. Then, return the baskets to the Ninja foodi air fryer.

Now, you can use it again ;)

Breakfast Sausages and Biscuits

 PREPARATION TIME
5 MINUTES

 COOKING TIME
20 MINUTES

 SERVINGS
2 PERSONS

Ingredients:

- 500 gm (1 lb.) pork sausage roll
- 1 can Pre-baked Biscuits
- Cooking oil in spray
- Salt and pepper to taste
- Butter and jam for the biscuits

Instructions:

1. Slice the pork sausage roll into 1.5-inch-thick slices and place four of them in basket number 1 of the Ninja Foodi 2-Basket Air Fryer. Do not overcrowd.
2. Cut the pre-baked biscuit dough into four biscuits of around 2-inches thick. Spray basket number 2 and place the biscuits.
3. Select the AIR FRY cooking function for Zone 1 and use the TEMP arrows to set the temperature to 200°C (390°F).
4. Use the TIME arrows to set the timer to 18 minutes.
5. Program the Zone 2 setting REHEAT cooking function, TEMP to 180°c (360°F) and TIME to 12 minutes.
6. Press SMART FINISH and START/PAUSE.
7. Zone 1 will begin air frying, and zone 2 will be on hold.
8. Press PAUSE at the 9-minute mark and flip the breakfast sausages using tongs. Unpause.
9. PAUSE again when four minutes remain to flip the biscuits. Finish the cooking process.
10. Serve and season the sausages with salt and pepper to taste, spread butter over the biscuits and serve them with your favourite jam!

Waffles and Bacon

PREPARATION TIME
5 MINUTES

COOKING TIME
11 MINUTES

SERVINGS
2 PERSONS

Ingredients:

- 2 Frozen waffles
- 4 thin-cut bacon slices
- Butter and maple syrup to taste

Instructions:

1. Spread the bacon into basket 1 of the Ninja Foodi 2-Basket Air Fryer without overlapping.
2. Place the frozen waffles in basket 2 without overlapping.
3. Select the function AIR FRY in Zone 1. Use the TEMP arrows to set the temperature 205°C (400°F) and use TIME to set it for 10 minutes.
4. Select Zone 2 and set the function AIR FRY, TEMP 180°C (360°F) and time for 10 minutes.
5. Select SMART FINISH and press START/ PAUSE.
6. Zone 1 will begin air frying, and zone 2 will be on hold.
7. PAUSE after six minutes and flip the waffles and bacon. Finish cooking.
8. Serve and enjoy with butter and a maple syrup drizzle.

Breakfast Burrito with Sweet Potato Fries and Salsa

 PREPARATION TIME
45 MINUTES

 COOKING TIME
30 MINUTES

 SERVINGS
2 PERSONS

Ingredients:

For the sweet potato fries:
- 2 sweet potatoes
- 2 tablespoons of olive oil
- 2 tablespoons cornflour
- Salt and pepper to taste

For the burritos:
- 2 wheat tortillas
- 1/2 cup black beans, cooked and drained
- 1/2 cup white rice, cooked
- 4 tbsp Cheddar cheese, grated

For the salsa:
- 2 ripe tomatoes
- 1/4 white onion
- 1 fistful cilantro leaves
- Juice of 1 lime
- Salt to taste

Instructions:

1. Peel the sweet potatoes and cut the tips. Cut lengthwise and then into canes.
2. Rinse the sweet potatoes with cold water and let them soak in water for half an hour. Drain and pat dry thoroughly.
3. In a mixing bowl, toss the sweet potatoes with olive oil, cornflour, salt and pepper. Set aside.
4. For the burritos, in a mixing b owl, incorporate the black beans, rice and cheddar cheese. Mix well.
5. Divide the mixture over the tortillas without overfilling and tuck tightly; first, roll the sides, then fold the edges.
6. Carefully transfer the fries into basket 1 of the Ninja Foodi 2-Basket Air Fryer.
7. Place the burritos in the basket 2.
8. Select the function AIR FRY in Zone 1. Use the TEMP arrows to set the temperature 205°C (400°F) and use TIME to set it for 30 minutes.
9. Select Zone 2 and set the function AIR FRY, TEMP 180°C (360°F) and time for 12 minutes.
10. Select SMART FINISH and press START/PAUSE.
11. Zone 1 will begin air frying, and zone 2 will be on hold.
12. Shake the sweet potato basket halfway through.
13. To make the salsa, finely dice the tomatoes and onion, chop the cilantro and toss with lime juice. Season with salt and enjoy.

Egg Souffle with Bacon Bits

 PREPARATION TIME
10 MINUTES

 COOKING TIME
10 MINUTES

 SERVINGS
2 PERSONS

Ingredients:

- 1 tbsp butter, softened
- 2 eggs
- 1/2 cup Cheddar cheese, grated
- 2 tbsp heavy cream
- Salt and pepper to taste
- 2 tbsp Cheddar cheese for grating
- 4 thin-cut bacon slices
- Optionally, your favourite veggies or mushrooms for the egg souffles.

Instructions:

1. Butter two ramekins and set aside.
2. In a mixing bowl, whisk the eggs, cheese and heavy cream. Season with salt and pepper. Pour the mixture into the ramekins. Incorporate the veggies if using.
3. Spread the bacon in basket 1 of the Ninja Foodi 2-Basket Air Fryer without overlapping.
4. Place the ramekins in the basket 2.
5. Select the function AIR FRY in Zone 1. Use the TEMP arrows to set the temperature 205ºC (400ºF) and use TIME to set it for 12 minutes.
6. Select Zone 2 and set the function AIR FRY, TEMP 150ºC (300ºF) and time for 10 minutes.
7. Select SMART FINISH and press START/ PAUSE.
8. PAUSE after six minutes and flip the bacon. Top the egg ramekins with extra cheese and finish cooking by pressing START/PAUSE again.
9. Before serving, chop the crispy bacon into bits and top the egg souffles with it.

French Toast Sticks with Caramelised Bananas

 PREPARATION TIME 15 MINUTES

 COOKING TIME 8 MINUTES

 SERVINGS 2 PERSONS

Ingredients:

- 4 bread slices.
- 2 eggs
- 2 tablespoons whole milk
- 1/2 tsp vanilla extract
- 2 bananas
- 6 tbsp sugar
- 3 tbsp cinnamon powder
- Whipped cream to taste.

Instructions:

1. Trim the bread slices and cut each in half to get two sticks per slice. Set aside.
2. Peel the bananas and cut them lengthwise and then in half to get four banana slices per banana.
3. In a mixing bowl, whisk the eggs ad incorporate the milk and vanilla extract. In a second bowl, combine the sugar and the cinnamon.
4. Dip the bread slices in the egg mixture and coat with the sugar mixture.
5. Dip the bananas slices in the same way.
6. Transfer the French toast into basket 1 of the Ninja Foodi 2-Basket Air Fryer. Do not overcrowd or overlap.
7. Place the bananas in the basket 2. Do not overcrowd.
8. Select the function AIR FRY in Zone 1. Use the TEMP arrows to set the temperature at 175ºC (350ºF) and use TIME to set it for 12 minutes.
9. Select Zone 2 and set the function AIR FRY, TEMP 190ºC (375ºF) and time for 10 minutes.
10. Select SMART FINISH and press START/PAUSE.
11. Remove from the baskets and serve the French toast and bananas with a dollop of whipped cream.

Whole Fish & Chips

 PREPARATION TIME
10 MINUTES

 COOKING TIME
20 MINUTES

 SERVINGS
1 PERSONS

Ingredients:

For the fish:
- 1 whole fish, around 1 lb.
- 1 tsp thyme or oregano
- Salt and pepper to taste
- 1 lemon wedge
- Cooking oil in spray

For the chips:
- 1 large potato
- 1/2 tsp paprika
- Salt and pepper to taste
- Cooking oil in spray

Instructions:

1. Gut and scale the fish if not already clean.
2. Spray the fish with cooking oil and rub it with your favourite dried herbs, salt and pepper. Place in basket No. 1 in the Ninja Foodi 2-Basket Air Fryer.
3. For the chips, cut the potato into thin slices with a mandoline slicer. Spray with cooking oil and toss with paprika, salt and pepper. Place in basket No. 2 with the crisper plate installed.
4. Select the AIR FRY cooking function for Zone 1 and use the TEMP arrows to set the temperature to 204°C (400°F).
5. Use the TIME arrows to set the timer to 20 minutes.
6. Press MATCH COOK and START/PAUSE. Both baskets will begin frying at the same time.
7. Press PAUSE at the 10-minute mark, flip the whole fish and shake basket No.2. Resume cooking.
8. Serve the fried whole fish with a side of chips and a lemon wedge.

Garlic Shrimp & Onion Rings

PREPARATION TIME
25 MINUTES

COOKING TIME
22 MINUTES

SERVINGS
2 PERSONS

Ingredients:

For the shrimp:
- 1 lb. Shrimp, peeled and deveined
- 1/4 cup butter, softened
- 1 tsp garlic powder
- 1 tsp onion powder
- 1 tsp paprika
- 2 tbsp all-purpose flour
- Lemon wedges

For the onion rings:
- 1 large onion
- 1/2 cup all-purpose flour
- 4 tbsp corn starch
- 1 tsp baking powder
- 1 egg
- 1 cup breadcrumbs
- Cooking oil in spray

Instructions:

1. In a mixing bowl, combine the shrimp with the butter, garlic powder, onion powder, paprika and flour. Place in basket No.1 in the Ninja Foodi 2-Basket Air Fryer with the crisper plate installed.
2. For the onion rings, peel and cut the onion into rings. In a mixing bowl, combine the flour, cornstarch baking powder and a pinch of salt. Coat the onions in the flour mixture.
3. Whisk the egg in a small bowl and dip each onion ring. Then, coat them with breadcrumbs. Place the onion rings in basket No.2
4. Select the ROAST cooking function for Zone 1 and use the TEMP arrows to set the temperature to 200ºC (390ºF).
5. Use the TIME arrows to set the timer for 15 minutes.
6. Program the Zone 2 setting AIR FRY cooking function, TEMP to 190ºC (375ºF) and TIME to 22 minutes.
7. Press SMART FINISH and START/PAUSE.
8. Press PAUSE at the 11-minute mark and shake basket No.2. Resume cooking.
9. PAUSE again when 7 minutes remain to shake basket No.1. Resume cooking.
10. Serve the garlic shrimp with a side of onion rings, a lemon wedge and your favourite creamy dip.

Tuna Croquettes & Roasted Peppers

PREPARATION TIME
25 MINUTES

COOKING TIME
27 MINUTES

SERVINGS
2 PERSONS

Ingredients:

For the tuna croquettes:
- 1/4 cup butter
- 1/2 cup all-purpose flour
- 1 can tuna
- 1/4 white onion, minced
- 1 garlic clove, minced
- 1 tbsp chives, chopped
- 1 egg
- 2 cups breadcrumbs
- Salt and pepper to taste
- Cooking oil in spray

For the roasted peppers:
- 1 yellow bell pepper
- 1 green bell pepper
- 1/4 white onion
- 1 garlic, minced
- 1 tsp Worcestershire sauce
- Cooking oil in spray

Instructions:

1. For the croquettes, combine the flour and the egg to form a thick batter. Stir in the tuna, onion, garlic and chives. Season with salt and pepper to taste. Combine well and form 4 croquettes.
2. Dip the croquettes in the whisked egg and coat with breadcrumbs. Spray with cooking oil and place in basket No.1 in the Ninja Foodi 2-Basket Air Fryer with the crisper plate installed.
3. For the roasted peppers, devein the peppers and dice them. In a mixing bowl, spray with cooking oil and toss with the onion, garlic and Worcestershire sauce. Season to taste with salt and pepper. Place in basket No.2 with the crisper plate attached.
4. Select the BAKE cooking function for Zone 1 and use the TEMP arrows to set the temperature to 176°C (350°F).
5. Use the TIME arrows to set the timer to 20 minutes.
6. Program the Zone 2 setting ROAST cooking function, TEMP to 182°C (360°F) and TIME to 27 minutes.
7. Press SMART FINISH and START/PAUSE.
8. Press PAUSE at the 13-minute mark and shake basket No. 2. Resume cooking.
9. PAUSE again when 10 minutes remain to flip the croquettes. Resume cooking.
10. Serve the tuna croquettes with a side of roasted peppers and an optional side of white rice.

Breaded Sea Scallops and Tostones

 PREPARATION TIME
15 MINUTES

 COOKING TIME
35 MINUTES

 SERVINGS
2 PERSONS

Ingredients:

For the scallops:
- 6 sea scallops
- 4 tbsp all-purpose flour
- 1 egg
- Salt and pepper to taste
- 1/2 cup breadcrumbs
- Cooking oil in spray
- Lemon wedges

For the tostones:
- 1 green plantain
- Cooking oil in spray
- Salt to taste

Instructions:

1. Pat the scallops dry and coat them with all-purpose flour.
2. Whisk the egg in a small bowl and season with salt and pepper. Dip the scallops in the egg mixture and coat them with breadcrumbs. Spray with cooking oil and place in basket No. 1 in the Ninja Foodi 2-Basket Air Fryer with the crisper plate installed.
3. For the tostones, slice the plantain and use the bottom of a plate to press them 1 cm thin. Spray with cooking oil, sprinkle them with salt, and place them in basket No.2 with the crisper plate attached.
4. Select the BAKE cooking function for Zone 1 and use the TEMP arrows to set the temperature to 198°C (390°F).
5. Use the TIME arrows to set the timer to 13 minutes.
6. Program the Zone 2 setting ROAST cooking function, TEMP to 205°C (400°F) and TIME to 35 minutes.
7. Press SMART FINISH and START/PAUSE.
8. Press PAUSE at the 15-minute mark and shake basket No. 2. Resume cooking.
9. PAUSE again when 6 minutes remain to flip the scallops. Resume cooking.
10. Serve the breaded sea scallops with a side of tropical tostones and lemon wedges.

Glazed Salmon & Zucchini Chips

 PREPARATION TIME
20 MINUTES

 COOKING TIME
28 MINUTES

 SERVINGS
2 PERSONS

Ingredients:

For the salmon:
- 2 250gr. salmon fillets
- 1/2 cup olive oil
- 1/3 cup molasses
- 1 garlic clove, minced
- 1 tsp grated lemon zest

For the zucchini chips:
- 1 large zucchini
- 1 tsp dried oregano
- 1/2 tsp garlic powder
- Salt and pepper to taste
- Cooking oil in spray

Instructions:

1. In a bowl, combine the olive oil, molasses, garlic and lemon zest. Brush the salmon fillets, shake the excess and place in basket No. 1 in the Ninja Foodi 2-Basket Air Fryer with the crisper plate attached.
2. For the zucchini chips, slice the zucchini, pray with cooking oil and toss with the oregano, garlic powder, salt and pepper.
3. Place them in basket No.2 with the crisper plate attached.
4. Select the ROAST cooking function for Zone 1 and use the TEMP arrows to set the temperature to 198ºC (390ºF).
5. Use the TIME arrows to set the timer for 15 minutes.
6. Program the Zone 2 setting ROAST cooking function, TEMP to 198ºC (390ºF) and TIME to 28 minutes.
7. Press SMART FINISH and START/PAUSE.
8. Press PAUSE at the 15-minute mark and shake basket No. 2. Resume cooking.
9. Serve the glazed salmon with a side of zucchini chips.

Crab Cakes & Southern Green Beans

PREPARATION TIME
20 MINUTES

COOKING TIME
15 MINUTES

SERVINGS
2 PERSONS

Ingredients:

For the crab cakes:
- 1 lb. Crab meat
- 1/2 cup breadcrumbs
- 2 tbsp fresh parsley
- 1 tsp Old Bay Seasoning
- Cooking oil in spray

For the green beans:
- 1 lb. Green beans
- 1 tbsp Cajun seasoning
- 1 garlic clove, minced
- Salt and pepper to taste
- Cooking oil in spray

Instructions:

1. In a mixing bowl, combine the crab meat, breadcrumbs, fresh parsley and old bay seasoning. Form cakes with the mixture, spray them with cooking oil and place them in basket No. 1 in the Ninja Foodi 2-Basket Air Fryer with the crisper plate attached.
2. For the green beans, spray them with cooking oil and toss them with the Cajun seasoning, garlic, salt and pepper. Place them in basket No.2 with the crisper plate attached.
3. Select the AIR FRY cooking function for Zone 1 and use the TEMP arrows to set the temperature to 198°C (390°F).
4. Use the TIME arrows to set the timer for 15 minutes.
5. Press MATCH COOK and START/PAUSE. Both baskets will begin frying at the same time.
6. Press PAUSE at the 7-minute mark, flip the crab cakes and shake basket No. 2. Resume cooking.
7. Serve the crab cakes with a side of Southern green beans.

Lemon Pepper Shrimp & 5-Spice Wedges

 PREPARATION TIME
25 MINUTES

 COOKING TIME
22 MINUTES

 SERVINGS
2 PERSONS

Ingredients:

For the shrimp:
- 1 lb. Shrimp, peeled and deveined
- 1/4 cup butter, softened
- 1 tsp garlic powder
- 1 tsp onion powder
- 1 tsp black pepper
- 1 tsp grated lemon zest
- 2 tbsp all-purpose flour
- Lemon wedges

For the potato wedges:
- 2 Russet potatoes cut in 2.5cm wedges
- 1 tbsp Chines 5-spice mix
- 1/2 tsp salt
- 1/2 tsp black pepper
- Cooking oil in spray

Instructions:

1. In a mixing bowl, combine the shrimp with the butter, garlic powder, onion powder, lemon zest, black pepper and flour. Place in basket No.1 in the Ninja Foodi 2-Basket Air Fryer with the crisper plate installed.
2. For the potato wedges, coat the wedges with cooking oil in spray and toss with the 5-spice mix, salt and pepper. Place in basket No.2.
3. Select the ROAST cooking function for Zone 1 and use the TEMP arrows to set the temperature to 200°C (390°F).
4. Use the TIME arrows to set the timer for 15 minutes.
5. Program the Zone 2 setting AIR FRY cooking function, TEMP to 180°C (360°F) and TIME to 20 minutes.
6. Press SMART FINISH and START/PAUSE.
7. Press PAUSE at the 10-minute mark and shake basket No.2. Resume cooking.
8. PAUSE again when 7 minutes remain to shake basket No.1. Resume cooking.
9. Serve the lemon-pepper shrimp with a side of potato wedges and a lemon wedge.

Breaded Shrimp & Broccoli Parmesan

 PREPARATION TIME
15 MINUTES

 COOKING TIME
13 MINUTES

 SERVINGS
2 PERSONS

Ingredients:

For the breaded shrimp:
- ½ cup all purpose flour
- 12 shrimp, peeled and deveined
- 1 egg
- 1/2 cup breadcrumbs
- Salt and pepper to taste
- Cooking oil in spray
- Lemon wedges

For the broccoli:
- 14 oz broccoli, cut in 2.5cm florets
- 1/2 tsp black pepper
- 4 tbsp grated Parmesan
- Cooking oil in spray

Instructions:

1. Pat the shrimp dry and coat with all-purpose flour.
2. Whisk the egg in a small bowl and season with salt and pepper. Dip the shrimp in the egg mixture and coat it with breadcrumbs.
3. Spray the shrimp with cooking oil and place it in basket No. 1 in the Ninja Foodi 2-Basket Air Fryer with the crisper plate installed.
4. In a mixing bowl, spray the broccoli florets with cooking oil and toss with the Parmesan and black pepper. Place in basket No.2.
5. Select the BAKE cooking function for Zone 1 and use the TEMP arrows to set the temperature to 198°C (390°F).
6. Use the TIME arrows to set the timer to 15 minutes.
7. Press MATCH COOK and START/PAUSE. Both baskets will begin frying at the same time.
8. Press PAUSE at the 7-minute mark and shake both baskets. Resume cooking.
9. Serve the shrimp with a side of broccoli and a lemon wedge.

Fish Sticks & Parmesan Carrots

 PREPARATION TIME
20 MINUTES

 COOKING TIME
25 MINUTES

 SERVINGS
2 PERSONS

Ingredients:

For the fish sticks:
- 1 lb. Cod fillets
- 1/2 cup all-purpose flour
- 1 egg
- 1/2 cup breadcrumbs
- Salt and pepper to taste
- Cooking oil in spray

For the parmesan carrots:
- 2 carrots
- 1 tbsp grated Parmesan
- 1 tbsp dried parsley
- Salt and pepper to taste
- Cooking oil in spray

Instructions:

1. Cut the fillets into strips. Pat them dry with a paper towel and coat them in all-purpose flour.
2. Whisk the egg in a bowl and season it with salt and pepper. Dip the fish sticks. Coat them in breadcrumbs and place them in basket No. 1 in the Ninja Foodi 2-Basket Air Fryer with the crisper plate installed.
3. Cut the carrots into canes, spray them with cooking oil and toss them with Parmesan, parsley, salt and pepper. Place in basket No. 2.
4. Select the AIR FRY cooking function for Zone 1 and use the TEMP arrows to set the temperature to 198°C (390°F).
5. Use the TIME arrows to set the timer for 14 minutes.
6. Program the Zone 2 setting ROAST cooking function, TEMP to 198°C (390°F) and TIME to 25 minutes.
7. Press SMART FINISH and START/PAUSE.
8. Press PAUSE at the 12-minute mark and shake basket No.2. Resume cooking.
9. PAUSE again when 7 minutes remain to flip the fish sticks. Resume cooking.
10. Serve the fish sticks with a side of Parmesan carrots and a lemon wedge.

Cajun Shrimp Broil & Sweet Corn

PREPARATION TIME
15 MINUTES

COOKING TIME
15 MINUTES

SERVINGS
2 PERSONS

Ingredients:

For the shrimp:
- 1 lb. Shrimp, unpeeled
- 1/4 cup butter, softened
- 1 tsp garlic powder
- 1 tsp onion powder
- 1 tbsp Cajun spices
- 2 tbsp all-purpose flour
- Lemon wedges

For the Sweet corn:
- 2 yellow corns on the cob
- 1 tsp paprika
- Cooking oil in spray
- 2 tsp butter

Instructions:

1. In a mixing bowl, combine the shrimp with the butter, garlic powder, onion powder, Cajun spices and flour. Place in basket No.1 in the Ninja Foodi 2-Basket Air Fryer with the crisper plate installed.
2. Spray the corn on the cob with cooking oil, sprinkle with paprika and place on basket No. 2.
3. Select the ROAST cooking function for Zone 1 and use the TEMP arrows to set the temperature to 200°C (390°F).
4. Use the TIME arrows to set the timer for 15 minutes.
5. Press MATCH COOK and START/PAUSE. Both baskets will begin frying at the same time.
6. Press PAUSE at the 7-minute mark, turn the corn and shake basket No.1. Resume cooking.
7. Serve the Cajun shrimp with a side of sweet corn with a dab of butter. Peel the shrimp as you go and enjoy!

Cauliflower Cheese

 PREPARATION TIME
10 MINUTES

 COOKING TIME
15 MINUTES

 SERVINGS
2 PERSONS

Ingredients:

- 2 cups cauliflower florets
- Cooking oil in spray
- Salt and pepper to taste
- 1/2 cup onion, minced
- 1/2 cup bacon, diced
- 1/2 cup cheddar cheese

Instructions:

1. Spray the cauliflower florets and onion with cooking oil and toss with salt and pepper. Place in basket No.1 in the Ninja Foodi 2-Basket Air Fryer with the crisper plate installed.
2. Place the bacon bits in basket No.2 with the crisper plate installed.
3. Select the ROAST cooking function for Zone 1 and use the TEMP arrows to set the temperature to 200°C (390°F).
4. Use the TIME arrows to set the timer for 15 minutes.
5. Program the Zone 2 setting AIR FRY cooking function, TEMP to 176°C (350°F) and TIME to 12 minutes.
6. Press SMART FINISH and START/PAUSE.
7. Press PAUSE at the 7-minute mark and shake basket No.1. Resume cooking.
8. PAUSE again when 5 minutes remain to shake basket No.2. Resume cooking.
9. Combine the cauliflower and the bacon, top with cheese and stir until the cheese melts. Optionally, garnish with chopped chives. Serve with pork and poultry dishes.

Bubble & Squeak

PREPARATION TIME
10 MINUTES

COOKING TIME
15 MINUTES

SERVINGS
2 PERSONS

Ingredients:

- 2 cups leftover mashed potatoes
- 1 cup leftover cabbage
- 1/2 cup leftover shredded meat (optional)
- 4 tbsp cheddar cheese
- 1/2 tsp dried thyme
- 1/2 tsp dried rosemary
- Salt and pepper to taste

Instructions:

1. Combine all the ingredients in a mixing bowl and season with salt and pepper; pour into basket No. 1 in the Ninja Foodi 2-Basket Air Fryer.
2. Select the REHEAT cooking function for Zone 1 and use the TEMP arrows to set the temperature to 200°C (390°F).
3. Use the TIME arrows to set the timer for 15 minutes.
4. Press START/PAUSE.
5. Press PAUSE at the 7-minute mark and stir the contents in basket No.1. Resume cooking.
6. Serve the bubble & squeak; it should be firm enough to slice in half.

Mushy Peas

 PREPARATION TIME
5 MINUTES

 COOKING TIME
40 MINUTES

 SERVINGS
2 PERSONS

Ingredients:

- 2 cups frozen green peas
- 1/2 cup heavy cream
- 1 tbsp butter
- Salt and pepper to taste
- Cooking oil in spray

Instructions:

1. Spray with cooking oil and place the frozen peas in basket No. 1 in the Ninja Foodi 2-Basket Air Fryer.
2. Select the ROAST cooking function for Zone 1 and use the TEMP arrows to set the temperature to 176ºC (350ºF).
3. Use the TIME arrows to set the timer to 30 minutes.
4. Press START/PAUSE.
5. Press PAUSE at the 15-minute mark and shake the basket. Resume cooking.
6. Remove the chickpeas and pour them into a mixing bowl. Combine with heavy cream, butter and season with salt and pepper.
7. Mash to the desired texture and serve as a perfect side dish for hearty meals.

Scottish Stovies

PREPARATION TIME
10 MINUTES

COOKING TIME
25 MINUTES

SERVINGS
2 PERSONS

Ingredients:

- 1/2 cup leftover roast beef
- 1/2 cup leftover roast potatoes
- 2 tbsp leftover beef dripping
- 1 carrot
- 1/4 yellow onion

Instructions:

1. Dice the onion. Peel and slice the carrots. Spray with cooking oil, season with salt and pepper and place in basket No. 1 in the Ninja Foodi 2-Basket Air Fryer with the crisper plate installed..
2. Select the ROAST cooking function for Zone 1 and use the TEMP arrows to set the temperature to 200ºC (390ºF).
3. Use the TIME arrows to set the timer to 25 minutes.
4. Combine the leftover beef roast, potatoes and leftover dripping and pour into basket No2.
5. Program the Zone 2 setting REHEAT cooking function, TEMP to 190ºC (375ºF) and TIME to 15 minutes.
6. Press SMART FINISH and START/PAUSE.
7. Press PAUSE at the 12-minute mark and shake basket No.1. Resume cooking.
8. PAUSE again when 7 minutes remain to stir the contents in basket No.2. Resume cooking.
9. Combine the contents of both baskets and serve.

Scottish Clapshot

 PREPARATION TIME
10 MINUTES

 COOKING TIME
30 MINUTES

 SERVINGS
2 PERSONS

Ingredients:

- 2 potatoes, diced
- 1/2 cup turnips, peeled and diced
- 1/2 cup carrots, peeled and diced
- Cooking oil in spray
- Salt and pepper to taste
- 2 tbsp butter

Instructions:

1. In a mixing bowl, combine the potatoes, turnips and carrots. Spray with cooking oil and season with salt and pepper. Place in basket No.1 in the Ninja Foodi 2-Basket Air Fryer.
2. Select the ROAST cooking function for Zone 1 and use the TEMP arrows to set the temperature to 204°C (400°F).
3. Use the TIME arrows to set the timer to 30 minutes.
4. Press START/PAUSE.
5. Press PAUSE at the 15-minute mark and shake basket No.1. Resume cooking.
6. Remove the vegetables from the air fryer, mash to the desired texture, combine with the butter and serve.

Vegetarian Glamorgan Sausages

 PREPARATION TIME
10 MINUTES

 COOKING TIME
15 MINUTES

 SERVINGS
2 PERSONS

Ingredients:

- 1/2 cup leeks, peeled and diced
- 1/2 cup breadcrumbs
- 1 tbsp Cheddar cheese
- 1 tbsp butter
- 1 tsp fresh parsley
- 1 tsp dried thyme
- 1 egg
- Salt and pepper to taste

Instructions:

1. In a mixing bowl, combine all the ingredients to form a firm dough. If too runny, add more breadcrumbs. Season with salt and pepper.
2. Shape 2 sausage patties and spray with cooking oil. Place in basket No 1. in the Ninja Foodi 2-Basket Air Fryer.
3. Select the AIR FRY cooking function for Zone 1 and use the TEMP arrows to set the temperature to 204°C (390°F).
4. Use the TIME arrows to set the timer to 15 minutes. For a larger batch, place sausages in both baskets and press MATCH COOK.
5. Press START/PAUSE.
6. Press PAUSE at the 7-minute mark and flip the sausage patties. Resume cooking.
7. Serve with red onion relish.

Scottish Rumbled thumps

 PREPARATION TIME
10 MINUTES

 COOKING TIME
15 MINUTES

 SERVINGS
2 PERSONS

Ingredients:

- 2 potatoes, peeled, boiled and grated
- 1/4 cup breadcrumbs
- 1/4 cup turnip, peeled, boiled and grated
- 1/4 cup cabbage
- 1 garlic clove, minced
- 1 tbsp Cheddar cheese, grated
- 1 tbsp butter
- Salt and pepper to taste
- Cooking oil in spray

Instructions:

1. In a mixing bowl, combine all the ingredients and form two bite-sized balls.
2. Spray with cooking oil and place in basket No. 1 in the Ninja Foodi 2-Basket Air Fryer.
3. Select the REHEAT cooking function for Zone 1 and use the TEMP arrows to set the temperature to 204°C (390°F).
4. Use the TIME arrows to set the timer to 15 minutes. For a larger batch, place extra rumbledethumps in basket No.2 and press MATCH COOK.
5. Press START/PAUSE.
6. Press PAUSE at the 7-minute mark and flip the rumbledethumps. Resume cooking.
7. Serve with a hearty stew.

Bulgarian Egg Scramble

 PREPARATION TIME
5 MINUTES

 COOKING TIME
6 MINUTES

 SERVINGS
2 PERSONS

Ingredients:

- 1/2 white onion, diced
- 1 bell pepper, diced
- 4 eggs
- 2 tbsp grated Cheddar cheese, grated
- 1 tsp herbs de Provence
- 1 tsp paprika
- Salt and pepper to taste

Instructions:

1. In an air fryer-safe pan, combine all the ingredients. Place in basket No. 1 in the Ninja Foodi 2-Basket Air Fryer.
2. Select the BAKE cooking function for Zone 1 and use the TEMP arrows to set the temperature to 150°C (300°F).
3. Use the TIME arrows to set the timer to 6 minutes. For a larger batch, place extra scrambled eggs into basket No.2 and press MATCH COOK.
4. Press START/PAUSE.
5. Press PAUSE at the 3-minute mark and scramble the egg mixture with a spoon. Resume cooking.
6. Serve with a slice of bread.

Veggie Karbanátky

PREPARATION TIME
15 MINUTES

COOKING TIME
15 MINUTES

SERVINGS
2 PERSONS

Ingredients:

- 1/4 cup carrot, grated
- 1/4 cup zucchini, grated
- 1 egg
- 1/4 white onion, minced
- 1 garlic clove, minced
- 1/4 cup parsley, chopped
- 2 tbsp all-purpose flour
- 1/2 tsp marjoram
- 1/2 cup fine breadcrumbs
- Cooking oil in Spray
- Salt and pepper to taste
- Chives, chopped as a garnish

Instructions:

1. Combine the carrot, zucchini, egg, onion, garlic, parsley, flour, marjoram and breadcrumbs in a mixing bowl.
2. Form patties and place in basket No.1 in the Ninja Foodi 2-Basket Air Fryer.
3. Select the AIR FRY cooking function for Zone 1 and use the TEMP arrows to set the temperature to 200ºC (390ºF).
4. Use the TIME arrows to set the timer to 15 minutes. For a larger batch, place extra karbanátky patties into basket No.2 and press MATCH COOK.
5. Press START/PAUSE.
6. Press PAUSE at the 7-minute mark and flip the patties. Resume cooking.
7. Serve with a green salad and garnish with chives.

Piperade

 PREPARATION TIME
10 MINUTES

 COOKING TIME
15 MINUTES

 SERVINGS
2 PERSONS

Ingredients:

- 2 plum tomatoes, peeled, deseeded and diced.
- 1 onion, sliced
- 1 green bell pepper, deseeded and diced
- 2 garlic cloves, minced
- 2 tbsp extra-virgin olive oil
- 1 tsp sugar
- ½ tsp hot paprika
- Salt and pepper to taste

Instructions:

1. Combine the tomatoes, onion, bell peppers and garlic in a mixing bowl. Toss with olive oil, season with sugar, paprika, salt and pepper.
2. Place in basket No. 1 in the Ninja Foodi 2-Basket Air Fryer.
3. Select the ROAST cooking function for Zone 1 and use the TEMP arrows to set the temperature to 200°C (390°F).
4. Use the TIME arrows to set the timer to 10 minutes. For a larger batch, place extra piperade into basket No.2 and press MATCH COOK.
5. Press START/PAUSE.
6. Press PAUSE at the 5-minute mark and stir. Resume cooking.
7. Serve with chicken, grilled meat or sausages.

Butter Steaks with Broccoli Parmesan

 PREPARATION TIME
10 MINUTES

 COOKING TIME
25 MINUTES

 SERVINGS
2 PERSONS

Ingredients:

- 2 6-oz ribeye steaks
- 4 tbsp butter, softened
- 1 garlic clove
- 1/2 Tsp dried rosemary
- 8 oz broccoli florets
- 2 tsp vegetable oil
- 2 tbsp Parmesan cheese, grated
- Salt and pepper to taste

Instructions:

1. Season the steaks with salt and pepper on all sides and let them sit until they reach room temperature.
2. In a mixing bowl, toss the broccoli florets with the oil, Parmesan and salt and pepper to taste.
3. Place the steaks in basket 1 and the broccoli in basket 2 with the crisper plate installed.
4. Select the ROAST cooking function for Zone 1 and use the TEMP arrows to set the temperature to 200°C (390°F).
5. Use the TIME arrows to set the timer to 20 minutes.
6. Program the Zone 2 setting AIRFRY cooking function, set TEMP to 390°F, and set TIME to 17 minutes.
7. Press SMART FINISH and START/PAUSE.
8. Once ten minutes have passed in Zone 1, PAUSE, and flip the steaks. Shake basket 2. Resume cooking.
9. Remove the steaks and let them rest over a platter. Remove the broccoli and set it aside.
10. Mince the garlic and add it into a small saucepan with the butter and rosemary. Cook briefly over a low flame on the stovetop until the garlic is fragrant.
11. Spoon the butter mixture over the steaks as they rest.
12. Serve the steaks with a side of broccoli Parmesan.

Meatballs with Sweet Potato Fries

 PREPARATION TIME
20 MINUTES

 COOKING TIME
31 MINUTES

 SERVINGS
2 PERSONS

Ingredients:

- 1 lb. ground beef
- 1 egg
- 3/4 cup breadcrumbs
- 2 tbsp onion, finely minced
- 1 garlic clove finely minced
- 2 sweet potatoes
- 1 tbsp paprika
- 1 tsp garlic powder
- Salt and pepper to taste
- 2 tbsp olive oil
- Cooking oil in spray

Instructions:

1. In a mixing bowl, combine the beef, egg, breadcrumbs, onion and garlic. Season with salt and pepper and form bite-sized balls with your palms. Set aside.
2. Cut the sweet potatoes into canes and toss them in a mixing bowl with 2 tablespoons of olive oil, paprika, garlic powder and salt and pepper to taste.
3. Spray basket 1 with cooking oil and place the meatballs without overcrowding.
4. Place the crisper plate in basket 2 and place the sweet potato fries.
5. Select the ROAST cooking function for Zone 1 and use the TEMP arrows to set the temperature to 205°C (400°F).
6. Use the TIME arrows to set the timer to 16 minutes.
7. Program the Zone 2 setting AIRFRY cooking function, TEMP to 180°c (390°F) and TIME to 31 minutes.
8. Press SMART FINISH and START/PAUSE.
9. When the Zone 1 time reaches 8 minutes, press START/PAUSE, remove the basket from the unit, and flip the meatballs. Shake the basket 2. Resume cooking.
10. When cooking is complete, transfer the meatballs onto the plates and serve with sweet potato fries.

Meatloaf with Carrot Fries

PREPARATION TIME
10 MINUTES

COOKING TIME
30 MINUTES

SERVINGS
2 PERSONS

Ingredients:

- ¾ pounds ground beef
- 1 egg
- ½ onion, chopped
- ½ cup milk
- ½ cup breadcrumbs
- 1 tbsp brown sugar
- 1 tbsp mustard
- 2 tbsp ketchup
- 4 carrots
- 2 tbsp olive oil
- 1 garlic clove, minced
- 2 Tbsp Parmesan, grated
- Salt and pepper to taste

Instructions:

1. In a mixing bowl, combine the ground beef, egg, onion, milk, breadcrumbs, brown sugar, mustard and ketchup. Season with salt and pepper to taste.
2. Once thoroughly mixed, spray cooking oil into an aluminum foil sheet and cover the meatloaf on all sides, leaving the top uncovered. Set aside.
3. Cut the carrots into canes and toss them in a mixing bowl with olive oil, garlic, Parmesan, salt and pepper.
4. Place the meatloaf in the basket 1. Insert the crisper plate in basket 2 and place the carrots.
5. Select the ROAST cooking function for Zone 1 and use the TEMP arrows to set the temperature to 200°C (390°F).
6. Use the TIME arrows to set the timer to 25 minutes.
7. Program the Zone 2 setting AIRFRY cooking function, TEMP to 180°c (390°F) and TIME to 30 minutes.
8. Press SMART FINISH and START/PAUSE.
9. When the Zone 2 time reaches 15 minutes, press START/PAUSE, remove the basket from the unit, and shake the basket. Resume cooking.
10. When cooking is complete, transfer the meatloaf into a platter, remove the foil and slice. Serve into plates with a side of carrot fries.

Korean BBQ Beef with Rosemary Potato Wedges

 PREPARATION TIME
10 MINUTES

 COOKING TIME
28 MINUTES

 SERVINGS
2 PERSONS

Ingredients:

- 1 lb. flank steak, sliced into strips
- 1/4 cup corn starch
- 2 potatoes, cut into wedges
- 1 tbsp cooking oil
- 1 tbsp rosemary, dried
- 1/2 cup soy sauce
- 3 tbsp rice vinegar
- 1 garlic clove, minced
- 1 1-inch piece of ginger, peeled and minced
- 2 tbsp brown sugar
- 1 tbsp chilli pepper flakes
- 1 tbsp corn starch (for the sauce)
- For garnish, chives and sesame seeds
- Cooking oil in spray
- Salt and pepper to taste

Instructions:

1. In a bowl, toss the flank steak with the corn starch and season with salt and pepper. Set aside.
2. In a second bowl, toss the potato wedges with the cooking oil and dried rosemary.
3. Place the flank steak in basket 1. Insert the crisper plate in basket 2 and place the potato wedges.
4. Select the AIRFRY cooking function for Zone 1 and use the TEMP arrows to set the temperature to 200ºC (390ºF).
5. Use the TIME arrows to set the timer to 18 minutes.
6. Program the Zone 2 setting AIRFRY cooking function, TEMP to 205ºc (400ºF) and TIME to 28 minutes.
7. Press SMART FINISH and START/PAUSE.
8. When the Zone 2 time reaches 14 minutes, press START/PAUSE, remove basket 1 and flip the steak. Shake the basket 2. Resume cooking.
9. In a small saucepan on the stovetop, mix the soy sauce, vinegar, garlic, ginger, brown sugar and pepper flakes. Heat over medium flame until just boiling, reduce the heat to low and add the corn starch. Reduce until thick.
10. To serve, remove the flank steak from basket 1, toss with the soy sauce mixture until fully coated and serve with a side of potato wedges. Garnish the Korean BBQ steak with sesame seeds and chopped chives.

Beef Roast with Potato Hay

 PREPARATION TIME
20 MINUTES

 COOKING TIME
1 HOUR 8 MINUTES

 SERVINGS
2 PERSONS

Ingredients:

- 1 lb. chuck roast or brisket
- 2 tbsp butter, softened
- 1 tbsp thyme, dried
- 2 potatoes
- Salt and pepper to taste
- Cooking oil in spray

Instructions:

1. Pat the roast dry with a paper towel.
2. Spray basket 1 with cooking oil and insert the crisper plate. Place the roast for searing.
3. Select the AIRFRY cooking function for Zone 1 and use the TEMP arrows to set the temperature to 205°C (390°F), TIME 18 minutes. Pulse START/PAUSE.
4. In a small bowl, combine the softened butter with the thyme and season with salt and pepper to taste. Set aside.
5. Remove and cover the seared roast in foil on all sides, leaving the top open. Top the roast with the seasoned butter and place in basket 1. Make sure there's room for the air to circulate.
6. Spiralise the potatoes to make the hay and spray with cooking oil. Place in basket 2.
7. Select the ROAST cooking function for Zone 1 and use the TEMP arrows to set the temperature to 160°C (320°F).
8. Use the TIME arrows to set the timer to 50 minutes.
9. Program the Zone 2 setting AIRFRY cooking function, TEMP to 180°c (390°F) and TIME to 20 minutes.
10. Press SMART FINISH and START/PAUSE.
11. When the Zone 2 time reaches 10 minutes, press START/PAUSE, remove basket 2 and shake. Resume cooking.
12. Before removing the roast, use a meat thermometer to ensure the core temperature is 145°F or higher.
13. Remove the roast and hay potatoes. Slice the roast and serve with a side of hay.

lamb loin Chops with french fries

 PREPARATION TIME
30 MINUTES

 COOKING TIME
40 MINUTES

SERVINGS
2 PERSONS

Ingredients:

- 1 lb. lamb chops
- 1 tbsp rosemary, dried
- 1 lb. potatoes
- Cooking oil in spray
- 2 tsp butter.
- Salt and pepper to taste

Instructions:

1. Spray the lamb chops with cooking oil and season with rosemary, salt and pepper. Place in the basket 1.
2. Select the AIRFRY cooking function for Zone 1 and use the TEMP arrows to set the temperature to 205°C (390°F), TIME 10 minutes. Sear the chops. Flip halfway, pressing START/PAUSE.
3. For the fries, cut the potatoes into sticks and boil them in water for 10 minutes. Rinse with cold water, drain and pat dry. Spray with the cooking oil and season with salt and pepper to taste.
4. Once the chops have finished searing, change the setting for Zone 1 to ROAST and use the TEMP arrows to set the temperature to 160°C (320°F). Adjust TIME to 20 minutes.
5. Place the fries into basket 2 and select AIRFRY, TEMP at 205°C (400°F), TIME 30 minutes.
6. Press SMART FINISH and START/PAUSE.
7. Once Zone 2 marks 15 minutes, press START/PAUSE, flip the lamb chops and shake the fries basket. Resume cooking.
8. Serve the chops with a dab of butter and a side of fries.

Roast lamb with Corn on the Cob

PREPARATION TIME
15 MINUTES

COOKING TIME
30 MINUTES

SERVINGS
2 PERSONS

Ingredients:

- 1 lb. lamb leg roast
- 1 tsp rosemary, dried
- 1 tsp thyme, dried
- 2 ears of corn
- 2 tbsp butter
- Salt and pepper to taste
- Cooking oil in spray

Instructions:

1. Spray the leg roast on all sides and rub with cooking oil, coat with rosemary, thyme, salt and pepper.
2. Place the lamb in basket 1.
3. Spray the ears of corn with cooking oil and place in basket 2.
4. Select the ROAST cooking function for Zone 1 and use the TEMP arrows to set the temperature to 182°C (360°F).
5. Use the TIME arrows to set the timer to 30 minutes.
6. Program the Zone 2 setting AIRFRY cooking function, TEMP to 188°c (370°F) and TIME to 16 minutes.
7. Press SMART FINISH and START/PAUSE.
8. Before removing the roast, check the inner temperature with a thermometer. Aim for 63°C (145°F).
9. Slice the lamb roast and serve it with an ear of corn. Spread the butter into the corn and season with extra salt and pepper.

Herb-Crusted Rack of lamb with Green Beans

 PREPARATION TIME
15 MINUTES

 COOKING TIME
18 MINUTES

 SERVINGS
2 PERSONS

Ingredients:

- 1 rack of lamb (6 ribs)
- 1 tbsp thyme
- 1 tbsp rosemary
- 1 tbsp oregano
- 1 garlic clove, minced
- 2 tbsp olive oil
- 1 lb. green beans
- Cooking oil in spray
- Salt and pepper to taste

Instructions:

1. In a small bowl, combine the olive oil and the dried herbs.
2. Rub the rack of lamb with the herb mixture and place it in basket 1.
3. Spray the green beans with cooking oil and toss with salt and pepper to taste. Place the green beans in basket 2.
4. Select the ROAST cooking function for Zone 1 and use the TEMP arrows to set the temperature to 182°C (360°F).
5. Use the TIME arrows to set the timer to 18 minutes.
6. Program the Zone 2 setting AIRFRY cooking function, TEMP to 198°c (390°F) and TIME to 10 minutes.
7. Press SMART FINISH and START/PAUSE.
8. Pause when Zone 2 marks 5 minutes and shake the basket. Resume cooking.
9. Check the lamb's temperature with a thermometer; it should reach 62°C (145°F) for rare.
10. Slice the rack of lamb and serve the chops with a side of green beans.

leg of lamb with Brussels Sprouts

 PREPARATION TIME
10 MINUTES

 COOKING TIME
40 MINUTES

 SERVINGS
2 PERSONS

Ingredients:

- 1 lb. Leg of lamb
- 1 lb. Brussels sprouts
- 1 tbsp olive oil
- 1 garlic clove, minced
- 2 tbsp Parmesan, grated
- Salt and pepper to taste
- Cooking oil in spray

Instructions:

1. Cut the Brussels sprouts in half and toss with the olive oil, minced garlic, salt and pepper. Place in basket 2 with the crisper plate equipped.
2. Spray the leg of lamb with cooking spray and rub with salt and pepper. Place on the basket 1.
3. Select the ROAST cooking function for Zone 1 and use the TEMP arrows to set the temperature to 182°C (360°F).
4. Use the TIME arrows to set the timer to 40 minutes.
5. Program the Zone 2 setting ROAST cooking function, TEMP to 190°c (375°F) and TIME to 15 minutes.
6. Press SMART FINISH and START/PAUSE.
7. Stop the timer when Zone 2 reaches 7-8 minutes and shake basket 2.
8. Check the lamb temperature with a thermometer aiming for 63°C (145°F).
9. Carve and serve the leg of lamb with a side of Brussels sprouts and sprinkle them with Parmesan.

lamb Meatballs with Mushrooms

 PREPARATION TIME
20 MINUTES

 COOKING TIME
15 MINUTES

 SERVINGS
2 PERSONS

Ingredients:

- 1 lb. ground lamb
- 1/4 onion, minced
- 1 garlic clove, minced
- 1 tsp cumin, powdered
- 1 tsp parsley, fresh
- 1/2 teaspoon ground cinnamon
- 400 grams button or cremini mushrooms, sliced
- 2 tbsp soy sauce

For the tzatziki sauce (optional):
- 1 cup Greek yoghurt
- 1/2 cucumber, finely diced
- 1 garlic clove, minced
- 1 tbsp lemon juice
- 1 tsp dill

Instructions:

1. In a mixing bowl, combine the ground lamb with the onion, garlic, cumin powder, cinnamon and parsley.
2. Roll bite-sized meatballs. Spray basket 1 with cooking oil and place the meatballs in basket 1.
3. Toss the sliced mushrooms with the soy sauce, drain any excess liquid and place in basket 2 with the crisper plate set up.
4. Select the AIR BROIL cooking function for Zone 1 and use the TEMP arrows to set the temperature to 182°C (360°F).
5. Use the TIME arrows to set the timer to 15 minutes.
6. Press MATCH COOK to copy the settings to Zone 2.
7. Press START/PAUSE.
8. Stop the timer halfway and shake the basket 2. Flip the meatballs with silicone tongs.
9. Make the tzatziki sauce combining the yoghurt, cucumber, garlic, lemon juice and dill. Refrigerate until ready to serve.
10. Serve the meatballs with a side of mushrooms. Serve with a side of creamy tzatziki sauce.

Bratwurst Bites with Garlic Potatoes

 PREPARATION TIME
15 MINUTES

 COOKING TIME
28 MINUTES

 SERVINGS
2 PERSONS

Ingredients:

- 2 large bratwursts
- 1 lb. baby potatoes, cut in half
- 2 tbsp olive oil
- 1 garlic clove, minced
- 1 tsp rosemary, dried
- Honey mustard to taste
- Salt and pepper to taste

Instructions:

1. Slice the bratwursts and place them in basket 1 with the crisper plate adjusted without overcrowding.
2. Toss the halved baby potatoes with olive oil, garlic, rosemary, salt and pepper and place in basket 2 with the crisper plate adjusted.
3. Select the ROAST cooking function for Zone 1 and use the TEMP arrows to set the temperature to 205°C (400°F).
4. Use the TIME arrows to set the timer to 12 minutes.
5. Program the Zone 2 setting AIRFRY cooking function, TEMP to 205°C (400°F) and TIME to 28 minutes.
6. Press SMART FINISH and START/PAUSE.
7. Stop the timer when Zone 2 reaches 14 minutes and shake both baskets. Resume cooking.
8. Serve the bratwurst bites with a side of garlic potatoes and a dab of honey mustard.

Pork Chops with Cauliflower Bites

PREPARATION TIME
15 MINUTES

COOKING TIME
15 MINUTES

SERVINGS
2 PERSONS

Ingredients:

- 1 lb. bone-in pork chops
- 1 cup cauliflower florets
- 1 tbsp olive oil
- 1/2 tsp paprika
- 1/2 tsp garlic powder
- 1/2 tsp onion powder
- Cooking oil in spray
- Salt and pepper to taste.

Instructions:

1. For the cauliflower florets, toss them in olive oil with paprika, garlic powder and onion powder. Place in basket 2 with the crisper plate attached.
2. For the pork chops, spray on both sides with cooking oil and rub with salt and pepper. Place on the basket 1.
3. Select the AIRFRY cooking function for Zone 1 and use the TEMP arrows to set the temperature to 205°C (400°F).
4. Use the TIME arrows to set the timer to 13 minutes.
5. Program the Zone 2 setting AIRFRY cooking function, TEMP to 200°C (390°F) and TIME to 15 minutes.
6. Press SMART FINISH and START/PAUSE.
7. Stop the timer when Zone 2 reaches 7-8 minutes and shake basket 2. Flip the pork chops. Resume cooking.
8. Serve the pork chops with a side of cauliflower bites and a tossed salad.

Glazed Pork Loin Roast with Asparagus

 PREPARATION TIME
10 MINUTES

 COOKING TIME
45 MINUTES

 SERVINGS
2 PERSONS

Ingredients:

- 1 lb. Pork loin, boneless, sliced
- 2 tbsp honey
- 2 tbsp mustard
- 1 tsp rosemary, dried
- 1 pound asparagus
- 2 tsp olive oil
- Salt and pepper to taste

Instructions:

1. Combine the honey, mustard and rosemary in a bowl, season the sliced pork loin with salt and pepper and coat with the honey mustard mixture. Drip away any excess liquid and place the loin in basket 1.
2. For the asparagus, toss them with olive oil, salt and pepper and place them on basket 2.
3. Select the AIRFRY cooking function for Zone 1 and use the TEMP arrows to set the temperature to 182°C (360°F).
4. Use the TIME arrows to set the timer to 45 minutes.
5. Program the Zone 2 setting AIRFRY cooking function, TEMP to 205°C (400°F) and TIME to 10 minutes.
6. Press SMART FINISH and START/PAUSE.
7. Stop the timer when Zone 1 reaches 30 minutes and flip the pork loin and the asparagus. Resume cooking.
8. Serve the pork loin with a side of asparagus.

Pork Tenderloin with Bacon-Stuffed Mushrooms

 PREPARATION TIME
20 MINUTES

 COOKING TIME
30 MINUTES

 SERVINGS
2 PERSONS

Ingredients:

- 1 lb. pork tenderloin
- 1 tbsp salt
- 2 tbsp paprika
- 2 tbsp lemon pepper
- 1 tbsp garlic powder
- 1 tbsp onion powder
- 1 tsp ground black pepper
- Cooking oil in spray
- 6 cremini mushrooms
- 3 oz cream cheese
- 2 tbsp bacon crumbles

Instructions:

1. In a mixing bowl, combine the spices and rub the tenderloin on all sides. Spray basket 1 and place the tenderloin.
2. Cut the mushroom's stems and discard. In a mixing bowl, combine the cream cheese with the bacon crumbles and stuff the mushrooms. Spray the mushrooms with oil and arrange them in basket 2.
3. Select the ROAST cooking function for Zone 1 and use the TEMP arrows to set the temperature to 205°C (400°F).
4. Use the TIME arrows to set the timer to 30 minutes.
5. Program the Zone 2 setting AIRFRY cooking function, TEMP to 176°C (350°F) and TIME to 10 minutes.
6. Press SMART FINISH and START/PAUSE.
7. Slice the tenderloin and serve with a few stuffed mushrooms and a side of mashed potatoes.

Pork Belly and Carrots with Balsamic Glaze

 PREPARATION TIME
15 MINUTES

 COOKING TIME
35 MINUTES

 SERVINGS
2 PERSONS

Ingredients:

- 1 lb. Pork belly, cut into cubes
- 1 tbsp brown sugar
- 1 tsp onion powder
- 1 tsp garlic powder
- 1 lb. heirloom carrots of all colours
- 2 tbsp olive oil
- 2 tbsp balsamic vinegar
- 1 tbsp honey
- Cooking oil in spray
- Salt and pepper to taste

Instructions:

1. In a bowl, combine the brown sugar, onion powder and garlic powder. Spray the pork belly with cooking oil and toss with the spice mix. Spray basket 1 and arrange the pork belly into the basket.
2. In a mixing bowl, combine the balsamic vinegar, olive oil and honey. Toss the carrots in the balsamic glaze, drip the excess liquid and place in basket 2 with the crisper plate installed.
3. Select the AIRFRY cooking function for Zone 1 and use the TEMP arrows to set the temperature to 176°C (350°F).
4. Use the TIME arrows to set the timer to 35 minutes.
5. Program the Zone 2 setting AIRFRY cooking function, TEMP to 200°C (390°F) and TIME to 12 minutes.
6. Press SMART FINISH and START/PAUSE.
7. Stop the timer when zone 1 marks 20 minutes. Flip the pork belly and shake the basket 2. Resume cooking.
8. Serve the pork belly with a side of glazed carrots.

Fried Chicken & Waffles

 PREPARATION TIME
10 MINUTES

 COOKING TIME
22 MINUTES

 SERVINGS
2 PERSONS

Ingredients:

For the fried chicken:
- 2 chicken leg-and-thigh pieces
- 1 cup all-purpose flour
- 1/2 tsp salt
- 1/2 tsp black pepper
- 1 cup buttermilk

For the waffles:
- 2 frozen waffles
- Cooking oil in spray

Instructions:

1. Use paper towels to pat the chicken dry.
2. In a mixing bowl, combine the flour, salt and black pepper. Coat the chicken thoroughly and pat down the excess flour.
3. Place the chicken in basket number 1 of the Ninja Foodi 2-Basket Air Fryer.
4. Spray basket number 2 with oil and place the waffles.
5. Select the AIR FRY cooking function for Zone 1 and use the TEMP arrows to set the temperature to 200ºC (390ºF).
6. Use the TIME arrows to set the timer to 22 minutes.
7. Program the Zone 2 setting REHEAT cooking function, TEMP to 180ºC (360ºF) and TIME to 10 minutes.
8. Press SMART FINISH and START/PAUSE.
9. Press PAUSE at the 11-minute mark and flip the chicken using tongs. Resume cooking.
10. PAUSE again when 5 minutes remain to flip the waffles. Resume cooking.
11. Serve the chicken over the waffles and drizzle with honey.

Wings & Wedges

 PREPARATION TIME
15 MINUTES

 COOKING TIME
33 MINUTES

 SERVINGS
2 PERSONS

Ingredients:

For the chicken wings:
- 1 lb. chicken wings
- 1 tbsp baking powder
- 1 tsp paprika
- 1/2 tsp salt
- 1/2 tsp black pepper
- Sriracha or Buffalo sauce to taste

For the potato wedges:
- 2 Russet potatoes cut in 2.5cm wedges
- 1/2 tsp cayenne pepper
- 1/2 tsp dried parsley
- 1/2 tsp salt
- 1/2 tsp black pepper
- Cooking oil in spray

Instructions:

1. Use paper towels to pat the chicken wings dry.
2. In a mixing bowl, combine baking powder, paprika, salt and black pepper. Toss the wings until fully coated and spray with cooking oil.
3. Coat the potato wedges with cooking oil and toss with the cayenne pepper, dried parsley, salt and pepper.
4. Place the chicken in basket number 1 of the Ninja Foodi 2-Basket Air Fryer.
5. Spray basket number 2 and place the potato wedges.
6. Select the AIR FRY cooking function for Zone 1 and use the TEMP arrows to set the temperature to 200°C (390°F).
7. Use the TIME arrows to set the timer to 33 minutes.
8. Program the Zone 2 setting AIR FRY cooking function, TEMP to 180°C (360°F) and TIME to 20 minutes.
9. Press SMART FINISH and START/PAUSE.
10. Press PAUSE at the 16-minute mark and shake basket No. 1. Resume cooking.
11. PAUSE again when 10 minutes remain to shake basket No. 2. Resume cooking.
12. Toss the chicken wings with your favourite hot sauce and serve with a side of potato wedges.

Sticky Chicken Thighs & Roasted Broccoli

PREPARATION TIME
15 MINUTES

COOKING TIME
28 MINUTES

SERVINGS
2 PERSONS

Ingredients:

For the thighs:
- 4 chicken thighs, bone-in, with skin
- 1/2 cup soy sauce
- 2 tbsp mirin
- 2 tbsp brown sugar
- 1 garlic clove, minced
- 1 tsp powdered ginger
- 2 tbsp corn starch

For the broccoli:
- 14 oz broccoli, cut in 2.5cm florets
- 1 tsp salt
- 1/2 tsp black pepper
- Cooking oil in spray

Instructions:

1. In a small pot over a low flame on the stovetop, combine the soy sauce, mirin, brown sugar, garlic and ginger. Mix and bring to a boil. Once boiling, pour in the corn starch and remove from heat.
2. Spray the broccoli florets with oil and toss with salt and pepper.
3. Coat the chicken thighs with the sauce, shake the excess and place in basket No.1 of the Ninja Foodi 2-Basket Air Fryer.
4. Spray basket number 2 and place the broccoli.
5. Select the ROAST cooking function for Zone 1 and use the TEMP arrows to set the temperature to 200ºC (390ºF).
6. Use the TIME arrows to set the timer to 28 minutes.
7. Program the Zone 2 setting AIR FRY cooking function, TEMP to 200ºC (390ºF) and TIME to 9 minutes.
8. Press SMART FINISH and START/PAUSE.
9. Press PAUSE at the 14-minute mark and change the thighs position. Resume cooking.
10. PAUSE again when 3 minutes remain to shake basket No. 2. Resume cooking.
11. Serve the thighs, pour any remaining sauce over them and serve with a side of roasted broccoli.

Chicken Meatballs & Broccoli Parmesan

 PREPARATION TIME
15 MINUTES

 COOKING TIME
20 MINUTES

 SERVINGS
2 PERSONS

Ingredients:

For the meatballs:
- 1 pound ground chicken
- 1 egg
- 1/2 cup breadcrumbs
- 1/2 cup grated Parmesan
- 1/2 tsp garlic powder
- 1/2 tsp onion powder
- 1/2 tsp salt
- 1&2 tsp black pepper

For the broccoli:
- 14 oz broccoli, cut in 2.5cm florets
- 1/2 tsp black pepper
- 4 tbsp grated Parmesan
- Cooking oil in spray

Instructions:

1. Combine the ground chicken with the egg, breadcrumbs, Parmesan, garlic and onion powder in a mixing bowl. Season with salt and pepper and mix with your hands.
2. Form bite-sized meatballs and set them aside.
3. In a second mixing bowl, spray the broccoli florets, toss with Parmesan and black pepper.
4. Place the chicken meatballs in basket No.1 with the crisper plate installed in the Ninja Foodi 2-Basket Air Fryer.
5. Spray basket number 2 and place the broccoli.
6. Select the ROAST cooking function for Zone 1 and use the TEMP arrows to set the temperature to 175°C (350°F).
7. Use the TIME arrows to set the timer to 20 minutes.
8. Program the Zone 2 setting AIR FRY cooking function, TEMP to 200°C (390°F) and TIME to 9 minutes.
9. Press SMART FINISH and START/PAUSE.
10. Press PAUSE at the 10-minute mark and shake basket No. 1. Resume cooking.
11. PAUSE again when 3 minutes remain to shake basket No. 2. Resume cooking.
12. Serve the meatballs with a side of roasted broccoli. Optionally coat the meatballs with tomato sauce or serve them over pasta.

Chicken Dumplings & Garlic Zucchini

 PREPARATION TIME
20 MINUTES

 COOKING TIME
18 MINUTES

 SERVINGS
2 PERSONS

Ingredients:

For the dumplings:
- 8 dumpling wrappers
- 2 chicken thighs, ground
- 150 gm. Napa cabbage
- 1 tsp ginger powder
- 1 garlic clove, minced

For the zucchini:
- 1 large zucchini, diced
- 1 garlic clove, minced
- 1/2 tsp salt
- 1/2 tsp pepper
- Cooking oil in spray
- Soy sauce for dipping

Instructions:

1. In a mixing bowl, combine the ground chicken, cabbage, garlic and ginger powder. Mix well.
2. With damp fingers, fill the dumpling wrappers with the chicken mixture and pinch the edges. Place in basket No.1 of the Ninja Foodi 2-Basket Air Fryer. The crisper plate installed.
3. In a mixing bowl, combine the diced zucchini with the garlic, salt and pepper. Spray with cooking oil and toss to coat.
4. Place the diced zucchini in basket No.2.
5. Select the AIR FRY cooking function for Zone 1 and use the TEMP arrows to set the temperature to 190°C (380°F).
6. Use the TIME arrows to set the timer to 18 minutes.
7. Press MATCH COOK and START/PAUSE. Both baskets will begin to fry at the same time.
8. Press PAUSE at the 9-minute mark and flip the dumplings and shake the zucchini basket. Resume cooking.
9. Serve the dumplings with a side of fried zucchini and dip them in soy sauce. Optionally, garnish with chopped chives.

Hot Chicken & Thin-cut Fries

PREPARATION TIME
15 MINUTES

COOKING TIME
22 MINUTES

SERVINGS
2 PERSONS

Ingredients:

For the fried chicken:
- 2 chicken leg-and-thigh pieces
- 1 cup all-purpose flour
- 1 tbsp cayenne pepper
- 1 tbsp paprika
- 1/2 tsp salt
- 1/2 tsp black pepper
- 1 cup buttermilk

For the thin-cut fries:
- 2 Russet potatoes cut into thin canes
- Cooking oil in spray

Instructions:

1. Use paper towels to pat the chicken dry.
2. In a mixing bowl, combine the flour, cayenne pepper, paprika, salt and black pepper. Coat the chicken thoroughly and pat down the excess flour.
3. In a mixing bowl, spray the potatoes with cooking oil and toss to coat.
4. Place the chicken in basket number 1 of the Ninja Foodi 2-Basket Air Fryer.
5. Spray basket number 2 and place the fries.
6. Select the AIR FRY cooking function for Zone 1 and use the TEMP arrows to set the temperature to 200°C (390°F).
7. Use the TIME arrows to set the timer to 22 minutes.
8. Program the Zone 2 setting AIR FRY cooking function, TEMP to 180°C (360°F) and TIME to 20 minutes.
9. Press SMART FINISH and START/PAUSE.
10. Press PAUSE at the 11-minute mark and flip the chicken using tongs. Resume cooking.
11. PAUSE again when 10 minutes remain to shake the basket. Resume cooking.
12. Serve the chicken with a side of fries and plenty of napkins!

Chicken Parmesan & Vegetable Medley

 PREPARATION TIME
15 MINUTES

 COOKING TIME
20 MINUTES

 SERVINGS
2 PERSONS

Ingredients:

For the chicken:
- 2 chicken cutlets
- 1 egg
- 1/2 cup breadcrumbs
- 1/2 tsp salt
- 1/2 tsp pepper
- 1/2 tsp dried thyme

For the veggies:
- 1 medium sweet potato, diced
- 1 zucchini, diced
- 1 bell pepper, deveined and sliced
- 1 tsp Italian herbs

Instructions:

1. Whisk the egg in a bowl, mix the breadcrumbs with the salt, pepper and thyme. Place the breadcrumbs on a plate.
2. Coat the cutlets with egg and breadcrumbs. Place in basket number 1 of the Ninja Foodi 2-Basket Air Fryer.
3. In a mixing bowl, spray the vegetables and toss with the salt, pepper and Italian dried herbs. Place on basket No. 2 with the crisper plate fixed.
4. Select the AIR FRY cooking function for Zone 1 and use the TEMP arrows to set the temperature to 200°C (390°F).
5. Use the TIME arrows to set the timer to 20 minutes.
6. Program the Zone 2 setting ROAST cooking function, TEMP to 180°C (360°F) and TIME to 20 minutes.
7. Press SMART FINISH and START/PAUSE.
8. Press PAUSE at the 10-minute mark, flip the chicken using tongs, and shake the vegetable basket. Resume cooking.
9. Serve the chicken with a side of medley and drizzle with extra virgin olive oil.

Crispy Chicken Tacos & Corn on the Cob

PREPARATION TIME
20 MINUTES

COOKING TIME
20 MINUTES

SERVINGS
2 PERSONS

Ingredients:

For the tacos:
- 8 corn tortillas
- 1 lb. Chicken breast
- 1/4 white onion, finely diced
- 1 garlic clove, minced
- 1/2 tsp salt
- 1/2 tsp pepper

For the corn:
- 2 yellow corns on the cob
- Cooking oil in spray

Instructions:

1. Boil the chicken, let it cool and shred it with a pair of forks.
2. In a skillet, sauté the garlic and onion until fragrant and translucent. Add the chicken and stir until golden. Set aside.
3. In a skillet, gently heat the tortillas and fill them with the chicken. Roll them and insert a toothpick to keep them rolled.
4. Place the tacos in basket number 1 of the Ninja Foodi 2-Basket Air Fryer.
5. Spray the corn on the cob with cooking oil and place it on basket No. 2.
6. Select the AIR FRY cooking function for Zone 1 and use the TEMP arrows to set the temperature to 200ºC (390ºF).
7. Use the TIME arrows to set the timer to 20 minutes.
8. Program the Zone 2 setting ROAST cooking function, TEMP to 200ºC (390ºF) and TIME to 15 minutes.
9. Press SMART FINISH and START/PAUSE.
10. Press PAUSE at the 10-minute mark and flip the chicken tacos using tongs. Remove the toothpicks. Resume cooking.
11. PAUSE again when 7 minutes remain to turn the corn. Resume cooking.
12. Serve the chicken tacos with spicy salsa and an ear of golden corn on the cob with a mayo spread.

Curry Drumsticks & Masala Cauliflower

 PREPARATION TIME
10 MINUTES

 COOKING TIME
22 MINUTES

 SERVINGS
2 PERSONS

Ingredients:

For the chicken:
- 4 chicken drumsticks
- 1/4 cup butter, melted
- 1 tsp garlic powder
- 1 tsp paprika
- 1 tsp curry powder
- 1 tsp cumin

For the cauliflower:
- 14 oz broccoli, cut in 2.5cm florets
- 1 tsp salt
- 1/2 tsp black pepper
- 1 tbsp masala spice mix
- Cooking oil in spray

Instructions:

1. Tossing the drumsticks with melted butter, garlic, paprika, curry and cumin in a mixing bowl. Place the drumsticks in basket number 1 of the Ninja Foodi 2-Basket Air Fryer.
2. Spray the cauliflower with cooking oil and toss with salt, pepper and masala. Place on basket No. 2.
3. Select the AIR FRY cooking function for Zone 1 and use the TEMP arrows to set the temperature to 200ºC (390ºF).
4. Use the TIME arrows to set the timer to 22 minutes.
5. Program the Zone 2 setting AIR FRY cooking function, TEMP to 200ºC (390ºF) and TIME to 9 minutes.
6. Press SMART FINISH and START/PAUSE.
7. Press PAUSE at the 11-minute mark and flip the chicken drumsticks. Resume cooking.
8. PAUSE again when 3 minutes remain to shake basket No. 2. Resume cooking.
9. Serve the chicken drumsticks with a side of masala cauliflower and white rice.

Chicken Pockets & Garlic Potatoes

 PREPARATION TIME
30 MINUTES

 COOKING TIME
20 MINUTES

 SERVINGS
2 PERSONS

Ingredients:

For the chicken pockets:
- 1 lb chicken breast, diced
- 1/4 yellow onion, finely sliced
- 1 bell pepper, sliced
- 1 garlic clove, minced
- 8 oz cream cheese
- Salt and pepper to taste
- 1 sheet frozen puff pastry
- 1 egg

For the garlic potatoes:
- 1 lb. Baby red potatoes
- 1 tsp dried oregano
- 1 garlic clove, minced
- Cooking oil as needed
- Cooking oil in spray

Instructions:

1. In a large skillet with two tablespoons of cooking oil over a high flame, sauté the onion and garlic for 2-3 minutes. Incorporate the bell pepper and cook until slightly roasted.
2. Add the chicken and toss until cooked through.
3. Reduce the flame to low and fold in the cream cheese.
4. Unfold the puff pastry and cut it into four squares.
5. Crate pockets filled with the chicken and cream cheese filling. Pinch them closed and wash with whisked egg.
6. Place the chicken pockets in basket No. 1. of the Ninja Foodi 2-Basket Air Fryer.
7. Spray the baby potatoes with cooking oil and toss with minced garlic, salt, pepper and oregano. Place into basket No. 2.
8. Select the AIR FRY cooking function for Zone 1 and use the TEMP arrows to set the temperature to 200ºC (400ºF).
9. Use the TIME arrows to set the timer to 20 minutes.
10. Program the Zone 2 setting ROAST cooking function, TEMP to 200ºC (400ºF) and TIME to 20 minutes.
11. Press SMART FINISH and START/PAUSE.
12. Press PAUSE at the 10-minute mark and flip the chicken pockets. Shake basket No. 2 Resume cooking.
13. Serve the chicken pockets with a side of garlic potatoes.

Homemade Nuggets & Sweet Potato Tots

 PREPARATION TIME
25 MINUTES

 COOKING TIME
20 MINUTES

 SERVINGS
2 PERSONS

Ingredients:

For the nuggets:
- 1 tsp sweet paprika
- 1 tsp garlic powder
- 1 tsp onion powder
- Salt and pepper to taste
- 1 lb. chicken breast, boneless, skinless
- 1/2 cup buttermilk
- 1 cup all-purpose flour
- Cooking oil in spray

For the sweet potato tots:
- 2 sweet potatoes, boiled and peeled
- 1 tbsp potato starch
- Salt and pepper to taste

Instructions:

1. Cut the chicken into bite-sized pieces.
2. In a mixing bowl, use your hands to coat the chicken with paprika, garlic powder, onion powder, salt and pepper.
3. Pour in the buttermilk and let the chicken marinate for 30 minutes in the fridge.
4. Coat each chicken piece with the flour draining the excess buttermilk. Spray with cooking oil and place into basket No. 1 of the Ninja Foodi 2-Basket Air Fryer.
5. For the sweet potato tots, grate the sweet potatoes and toss them with the potato starch. Season to taste.
6. Use a spoon to shape bite-sized tots, spray with cooking oil and place into basket No 2 with the crisper plate installed.
7. Select the AIR FRY cooking function for Zone 1 and use the TEMP arrows to set the temperature to 200°C (390°F).
8. Use the TIME arrows to set the timer to 18 minutes.
9. Program the Zone 2 setting ROAST cooking function, TEMP to 190°C (375°F) and TIME to 20 minutes.
10. Press SMART FINISH and START/PAUSE.
11. Press PAUSE at the 10-minute mark and shake both baskets. Resume cooking.
12. Serve the chicken nuggets with a side of sweet potato tots and a side of ketchup or mayo.

Cordon Bleu & Mushrooms

 PREPARATION TIME
25 MINUTES

 COOKING TIME
35 MINUTES

 SERVINGS
2 PERSONS

Ingredients:

For the chicken:
- 2 chicken breast halves, boneless, skinless
- 4 slices Swiss cheese
- 4 slices ham
- 1 egg
- 2 tbsp all-purpose flour
- 1 tbsp coarse breadcrumbs

For the mushrooms:
- 1 cup diced mushrooms
- 1 tsp thyme
- Salt and pepper to taste
- Cooking oil in spray

Instructions:

1. Place two slices of cheese over two slices of ham and roll loosely. Repeat.
2. Cut the chicken breasts halfway and fill them with the rolled ham and cheese.
3. Coat the filled chicken breasts with flour and set them aside.
4. In a bowl, whisk the egg and coat the chicken breasts with egg. Coat again with the breadcrumbs and place in basket No.1 of the Ninja Foodi 2-Basket Air Fryer. Spray with cooking oil.
5. For the mushrooms, spray the sliced mushrooms with cooking oil and toss with the thyme, salt and pepper. Place in basket No.2. With the crisper plate installed.
6. Select the ROAST cooking function for Zone 1 and use the TEMP arrows to set the temperature to 200ºC (390ºF).
7. Use the TIME arrows to set the timer to 35 minutes.
8. Program the Zone 2 setting ROAST cooking function, TEMP to 200ºC (390ºF) and TIME to 15 minutes.
9. Press SMART FINISH and START/PAUSE.
10. Press PAUSE at the 15-minute mark, flip the chicken breasts. Resume cooking.
11. PAUSE again when 7 minutes remain to shake basket No. 2. Resume cooking.
12. Serve the cordon bleu with a side of mushrooms. Alternatively, bathe the chicken with a creamy sauce.

Turkey Breast & Brussels Sprouts

 PREPARATION TIME
15 MINUTES

 COOKING TIME
40 MINUTES

 SERVINGS
2 PERSONS

Ingredients:

For the turkey:
- 1 tsp paprika
- 1 tsp dried rosemary
- 1 tsp dried thyme
- 1 tsp garlic powder
- Salt and pepper to taste
- 1/2 stick butter, softened
- 2 lb. split turkey breast, boneless

For the Brussels sprouts:
- 1 lb. Brussels sprouts
- 1/2 tsp salt
- 1/2 tsp black pepper
- 1 garlic clove, minced
- Cooking oil in spray

Instructions:

1. In a small bowl, combine the paprika, rosemary, thyme, garlic, salt pepper and the softened butter.
2. Pat the turkey breast dry with paper towels and rub with the spice and butter mixture on all sides.
3. Place the turkey in basket No.1 of the Ninja Foodi 2-Basket Air Fryer.
4. For the Brussels sprouts, trim the sprouts ends and cut them in half. Spray with cooking oil and toss with salt, pepper and garlic. Place in basket No.2 with the crisper plate installed.
5. Select the ROAST cooking function for Zone 1 and use the TEMP arrows to set the temperature to 182°C (360°F).
6. Use the TIME arrows to set the timer to 40 minutes.
7. Program the Zone 2 setting AIR FRY cooking function, TEMP to 204°C (400°F) and TIME to 20 minutes.
8. Press SMART FINISH and START/PAUSE.
9. Press PAUSE at the 20-minute mark, flip the turkey breast. Resume cooking.
10. PAUSE again when 10 minutes remain to shake basket No. 2. Resume cooking.
11. Check the turkey's core temperature aiming at 165°F. Serve the turkey breast with a side of Brussels sprouts. Optionally, serve with brown gravy.

Cornish Hen & Stuffed Tomatoes

 PREPARATION TIME
20 MINUTES

 COOKING TIME
40 MINUTES

 SERVINGS
2 PERSONS

Ingredients:

For the Cornish hen:
- 1 Cornish hen
- 1/2 stick butter, softened
- 1 tsp dried rosemary
- 1 tsp dried thyme
- 1 tsp dried oregano
- 1/2 tsp garlic powder
- Salt and pepper to taste

For the stuffed tomatoes:
- 2 tomatoes
- 1/2 cup shredded mozzarella
- 1/2 cup breadcrumbs
- 1/4 cup fresh basil leaves
- 1 garlic clove, minced
- Salt and pepper to taste
- 2 tbsp grated Parmesan
- Cooking oil in spray

Instructions:

1. Rub the Cornish hen with the softened butter, thyme, rosemary, oregano and garlic powder. Place in basket No.1 of the Ninja Foodi 2-Basket Air Fryer.
2. For the stuffed tomatoes, cut the tomatoes tips and remove the pulp.
3. In a mixing bowl, combine the mozzarella, breadcrumbs, basil and garlic. Fill the tomatoes with the mixture.
4. Spray the tomatoes with cooking oil and place them in basket No.2.
5. Select the ROAST cooking function for Zone 1 and use the TEMP arrows to set the temperature to 182°C (360°F).
6. Use the TIME arrows to set the timer to 40 minutes.
7. Program the Zone 2 setting ROAST cooking function, TEMP to 198°C (390°F) and TIME to 15 minutes.
8. Press SMART FINISH and START/PAUSE.
9. Press PAUSE at the 20-minute mark, turn the Cornish hen. Resume cooking.
10. Check the Cornish hen's core temperature aiming at 165°F. Serve the hen with a roasted tomato and sprinkle it with Parmesan.

Turkey Meatballs & Asparagus

 PREPARATION TIME
15 MINUTES

 COOKING TIME
20 MINUTES

 SERVINGS
2 PERSONS

Ingredients:

For the turkey meatballs:
- 1 pound ground turkey
- 1 egg
- 1/2 cup breadcrumbs
- 1/2 cup grated Parmesan
- 1/2 tsp garlic powder
- 1/2 tsp onion powder
- 1/2 tsp salt
- 1/2 tsp black pepper

For the asparagus:
- 8 pc asparagus
- 1/2 tsp black pepper
- 2 tbsp grated Parmesan
- Cooking oil in spray

Instructions:

1. Combine the ground turkey with the egg, breadcrumbs, Parmesan, garlic and onion powder in a mixing bowl. Season with salt and pepper and mix with your hands.
2. For bite-sized meatballs and set them aside.
3. In a second mixing bowl, spray the asparagus, toss with Parmesan and black pepper.
4. Place the turkey meatballs in basket No.1 with the crisper plate installed in the Ninja Foodi 2-Basket Air Fryer.
5. Spray basket number 2 and place the asparagus.
6. Select the ROAST cooking function for Zone 1 and use the TEMP arrows to set the temperature to 175°C (350°F).
7. Use the TIME arrows to set the timer to 20 minutes.
8. Program the Zone 2 setting AIR FRY cooking function, TEMP to 200°C (390°F) and TIME to 9 minutes.
9. Press SMART FINISH and START/PAUSE.
10. Press PAUSE at the 10-minute mark and turn the meatballs. Resume cooking.
11. PAUSE again when 3 minutes remain to turn the asparagus. Resume cooking.
12. Serve the turkey meatballs with a side of asparagus and, optionally, a side of white rice.

Apple Pie

PREPARATION TIME
15 MINUTES

COOKING TIME
15 MINUTES

SERVINGS
2 PERSONS

Ingredients:

- 1 pie crust
- 1 apple, in small dices
- 2 tsp lemon juice
- 1 tbsp ground cinnamon
- 2 tbsp brown sugar
- 1/2 tsp vanilla extract
- 1 tbsp butter
- 1 egg
- Cooking oil in spray

Instructions:

1. Place the pie crust in an air fryer-safe pan. Press into the bottom with your fingers. Reserve pie crust for the pie topping.
2. Spray the pie crust with cooking oil.
3. In a mixing bowl, combine the apple, lemon juice, cinnamon, sugar, vanilla and butter. Pour into the pie crust.
4. Top the pie with the top pie crust layer and brush with whisked egg.
5. Place the pie pan in basket No. 1 in the Ninja Foodi 2-Basket Air Fryer.
6. Select the function BAKE in Zone 1. Use the TEMP arrows to set the temperature at 175ºC (350ºF) and use TIME to set it for 15 minutes.
7. Select START/PAUSE.
8. Serve and enjoy!

Twinkies

 PREPARATION TIME
10 MINUTES

 COOKING TIME
10 MINUTES

 SERVINGS
4 PERSONS

Ingredients:

- 4 Hostess Twinkies
- 1 can Crescent roll dough
- 1 tbsp confectioners' sugar

Instructions:

1. Roll the crescent roll on a floured surface, cut it into four squares large enough to wrap a twinkie. Place the Twinkies, seal the dough and place in the baskets of the Ninja Foodi 2-Basket Air Fryer.
2. Select the function BAKE in Zone 1. Use the TEMP arrows to set the temperature at 175°C (350°F) and use TIME to set it for 10 minutes.
3. Press MATCH COOK and START/PAUSE.
4. Press PAUSE at the 5-minute mark and turn the fried twinkies. Resume cooking.
5. Serve, dust with confectioner's sugar and enjoy!

Apple Fritters

 PREPARATION TIME
15 MINUTES

 COOKING TIME
15 MINUTES

 SERVINGS
6 PERSONS

Ingredients:

- 1 apple, diced
- 1/2 cup all-purpose flour
- 1 tbsp sugar
- 1/2 tsp baking powder
- 1/4 tsp salt
- 1/2 tsp cinnamon
- 1/4 cup milk
- 1 tbsp butter, softened
- 1 egg
- 2 tbsp confectioners' sugar

Instructions:

1. In a mixing bowl, combine the flour, sugar, baking powder, salt and cinnamon.
2. Pour in the milk, butter and egg. Mix well to form a dough.
3. Fold in the diced apples and form two bite-sized fritters.
4. Place in basket No.1 in the Ninja Foodi 2-Basket Air Fryer with the crisper plate installed.
5. Select the BAKE cooking function for Zone 1 and use the TEMP arrows to set the temperature to 176°C (350°F).
6. Use the TIME arrows to set the timer to 15 minutes.
7. Press START/PAUSE.
8. Press PAUSE at the 7-minute mark and flip the fritters. Resume cooking.
9. Dust with confectioners' sugar and serve.

Scottish Shortbread Sticks

 PREPARATION TIME
20 MINUTES

 COOKING TIME
18 MINUTES

 SERVINGS
12 PERSONS

Ingredients:

- 1/2 cups butter, softened
- 1/4 cup packed brown sugar
- 1 cup all-purpose flour

Instructions:

1. In a mixing bowl, combine the butter and the sugar and whisk until frothy. Pour in the flour and mix well to form a dough.
2. Flour a surface and knead the dough for 5-8 minutes, roll and cut into sticks.
3. Place the sticks in both baskets in the Ninja Foodi 2-Basket Air Fryer with the crisper plate installed.
4. Select the BAKE cooking function for Zone 1 and use the TEMP arrows to set the temperature to 176°C (350°F).
5. Use the TIME arrows to set the timer to 18 minutes.
6. Press MATCH COOK and START/PAUSE.
7. Press PAUSE at the 9-minute mark and shake the sticks. Resume cooking.
8. Serve with a cup of milk tea.

Chocolate Chip Cookies

 PREPARATION TIME
15 MINUTES

 COOKING TIME
20 MINUTES

 SERVINGS
10 COOKIES

Ingredients:

- 1/3 cup unsalted butter, softened
- 1/4 cup granulated sugar
- 1/4 cup packed brown sugar
- 1/2 tsp vanilla extract
- 1 egg
- 1/2 tsp salt
- 1/2 tsp baking soda
- 3/4 cups all-purpose flour
- 3/4 cups chocolate chips
- Cooking oil in spray

Instructions:

1. In a mixing bowl, combine the butter and sugar. Whisk until frothy.
2. Add the vanilla extract, egg, salt, baking soda, flour and chocolate chips. Combine to form a batter.
3. Line the Ninja Foodi 2-Basket Air Fryer baskets with parchment paper and use a spoon to scoop 4-5 cookies into every basket.
4. Select the BAKE cooking function for Zone 1 and use the TEMP arrows to set the temperature to 176ºC (350ºF).
5. Use the TIME arrows to set the timer to 10 minutes.
6. Press MATCH COOK and START/PAUSE.
7. Press PAUSE at the 5-minute mark to flatten and give shape to the cookies. Make sure they're not touching. Resume cooking.
8. Serve with a cold glass of milk.

Dehydrated Apples and Bananas

 PREPARATION TIME
10 MINUTES

 COOKING TIME
10 HOURS

 SERVINGS
1 CUP EACH

Ingredients:

- 2 apples
- Juice of 1 lemon
- 2 bananas

Instructions:

1. Core the apples and slice them into rings. Fill a small bowl with water and add the lemon juice. Rinse the apple slices and pat them dry. Set aside.
2. Cut the bananas at 0.5 cm slices.
3. Place the apple rings in basket No. 1 of the Ninja Foodi 2-Basket Air Fryer and place the bananas in basket No. 2.
4. Select the DEHYDRATE cooking function for Zone 1 and use the TEMP arrows to set the temperature to 57°C (135°F).
5. Use the TIME arrows to set the timer to 7 hours.
6. Select the DEHYDRATE cooking function for Zone 2 and use the TEMP arrows to set the temperature to 57°C (135°F). Use the TIME arrows to set the timer to 8 hours.
7. Press SMART FINISH and START/PAUSE.
8. After the time has passed, make sure the apples and bananas have adequately dehydrated. Add an extra hour at the same temperature if needed.

Dehydrated Asparagus and Eggplants

PREPARATION TIME
15 MINUTES

COOKING TIME
7 HOURS

SERVINGS
1 CUP EACH

Ingredients:

- 1 cup asparagus cut into 1 cm pieces.
- 1 cup eggplants cut into 1 cm pieces.

Instructions:

1. Boil a quart of water and blanche the asparagus and eggplants separately, 5 minutes each. Pat dry.
2. Place the asparagus in basket No. 1 of the Ninja Foodi 2-Basket Air Fryer and place the eggplants in basket No. 2.
3. Select the DEHYDRATE cooking function for Zone 1 and use the TEMP arrows to set the temperature to 57°C (135°F).
4. Use the TIME arrows to set the timer to 7 hours.
5. Press MATCH COOK and START/PAUSE.
6. After the time has passed, make sure the asparagus and eggplants have adequately dehydrated. Add an extra hour at the same temperature if needed.

Dehydrated Tomatoes and Mushrooms

PREPARATION TIME
15 MINUTES

COOKING TIME
7 HOURS

SERVINGS
1 CUP EACH

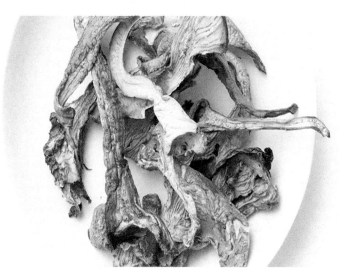

Ingredients:

- 1 cup tomatoes cut in 2 cm slices.
- 1 cup whole mushrooms brushed but not washed.

Instructions:

1. Place the tomatoes in basket No. 1 of the Ninja Foodi 2-Basket Air Fryer and place the mushrooms in basket No. 2.
2. Select the DEHYDRATE cooking function for Zone 1 and use the TEMP arrows to set the temperature to 57°C (135°F).
3. Use the TIME arrows to set the timer to 7 hours.
4. Press MATCH COOK and START/PAUSE.
5. After the time has passed, make sure the tomatoes and mushrooms have adequately dehydrated. Add an extra hour at the same temperature if needed.

Dehydrated Pineapples and Strawberries

 PREPARATION TIME
5 MINUTES

 COOKING TIME
7 HOURS

 SERVINGS
1 CUP EACH

Ingredients:

- 1 cup pineapples, peeled, cored and cut into 1 cm slices.
- 1 cup strawberries cut in half.

Instructions:

1. Place the pineapples in basket No. 1 of the Ninja Foodi 2-Basket Air Fryer and place the strawberries in basket No. 2.
2. Select the DEHYDRATE cooking function for Zone 1 and use the TEMP arrows to set the temperature to 57°C (135°F).
3. Use the TIME arrows to set the timer to 7 hours.
4. Press MATCH COOK and START/PAUSE.
5. After the time has passed, make sure the pineapples and strawberries have adequately dehydrated. Add an extra hour at the same temperature if needed.

Beef Jerky

PREPARATION TIME
10 MINUTES

COOKING TIME
6 HOURS

SERVINGS
150 GRAMS

Ingredients:

- 300 grams top round, bottom round, flank steak or skirt steak.
- 1/4 cup of soy sauce
- 2 tbsp of Worcestershire sauce
- Dash of liquid smoke flavouring
- 1/2 tsp hot pepper sauce
- 1/2 tsp garlic powder
- 1/2 tsp onion powder

Instructions:

1. Cut the beef into 0.5 cm slices, place them in a bowl and marinate the meat overnight with the rest of the ingredients covered with plastic film.
2. Drain and place the meat in basket No. 1 of the Ninja Foodi 2-Basket Air Fryer.
3. Select the DEHYDRATE cooking function for Zone 1 and use the TEMP arrows to set the temperature to 65°C (150°F). Use the TIME arrows to set the timer for 6 hours.
4. Press START/PAUSE.
5. After the time has passed, make sure the jerky has adequately dehydrated. Add an extra hour at the same temperature if needed.

Chicken Jerky

 PREPARATION TIME
10 MINUTES

 COOKING TIME
6 HOURS

 SERVINGS
150 GRAMS

Ingredients:

- 300 grams skinless, boneless chicken breast
- 1/4 cup of soy sauce
- 2 tbsp of Worcestershire sauce
- 2 tsp Teriyaki sauce
- 1/2 tsp dried parsley
- 1 tsp lemon juice
- 1/2 tsp garlic powder
- 1/2 tsp onion powder
- 1/2 tsp black pepper

Instructions:

1. Cut the chicken into 0.5 cm slices, place them in a bowl and marinate the chicken overnight with the rest of the ingredients covered with plastic film.
2. Drain and place the chicken in basket No. 1 of the Ninja Foodi 2-Basket Air Fryer.
3. Select the DEHYDRATE cooking function for Zone 1 and use the TEMP arrows to set the temperature to 65°C (150°F). Use the TIME arrows to set the timer for 6 hours.
4. Press START/PAUSE.
5. After the time has passed, make sure the jerky has adequately dehydrated. Add an extra hour at the same temperature if needed.

Turkey Jerky

PREPARATION TIME
10 MINUTES

COOKING TIME
6 HOURS

SERVINGS
150 GRAMS

Ingredients:

- 300 grams skinless, boneless turkey breast
- 1/4 cup of soy sauce
- 2 tbsp of Worcestershire sauce
- 1 tbsp brown sugar
- 1/2 tsp garlic powder
- 1/2 tsp onion powder
- 1 tsp liquid smoke
- 1/2 tsp black pepper

Instructions:

1. Cut the turkey in 0.5 cm slices, place them in a bowl and marinate the turkey overnight with the rest of the ingredients covered with plastic film.
2. Drain and place the turkey in basket No. 1 of the Ninja Foodi 2-Basket Air Fryer.
3. Select the DEHYDRATE cooking function for Zone 1 and use the TEMP arrows to set the temperature to 65°C (150°F). Use the TIME arrows to set the timer for 6 hours.
4. Press START/PAUSE.
5. After the time has passed, make sure the jerky has appropriately dehydrated. Add an extra hour at the same temperature if needed.

Salmon Jerky

 PREPARATION TIME
10 MINUTES

 COOKING TIME
14 HOURS

 SERVINGS
150 GRAMS

Ingredients:

- 300 grams salmon fillet
- 1/4 cup kosher salt
- 1/4 cup brown sugar
- 1/2 cup maple syrup

Instructions:

1. Cut the salmon into 0.5 cm slices, place them in a bowl and marinate the salmon overnight with the rest of the ingredients covered with plastic film.
2. Drain and place the salmon in basket No. 1 of the Ninja Foodi 2-Basket Air Fryer.
3. Select the DEHYDRATE cooking function for Zone 1 and use the TEMP arrows to set the temperature to 65°C (150°F).
4. Use the TIME arrows to set the timer to 4 hours.
5. Press START/PAUSE.
6. After the time has passed, make sure the jerky has adequately dehydrated. Add an extra hour at the same temperature if needed.

Bread

 PREPARATION TIME
50 MINUTES

 COOKING TIME
20 MINUTES

 SERVINGS
2 MINI LOAVES

Ingredients:

- 1 cup warm water
- 1 packet of instant yeast
- 2 tbsp sugar
- 3 cups all-purpose flour
- 1/4 cup vegetable oil
- 1 tsp salt
- Cooking oil in spray

Instructions:

1. In a bowl, combine the water, yeast and sugar. Pour in the flour, vegetable and salt. Combine until you get a smooth dough.
2. Flour a surface and knead for ten minutes. Form a ball and return to the mixing bowl. Cover with a kitchen towel and rest for 30 minutes.
3. Spray two pans fitted to the two Ninja Foodi 2-Basket Air Fryer baskets and divide the dough between them.
4. Select the BAKE cooking function for Zone 1 and use the TEMP arrows to set the temperature to 168°C (335°F). Use the TIME arrows to set the timer to 20 minutes.
5. Press MATCH COOK and START/PAUSE.
6. After 15 minutes have passed, check if the bread is cooked through. Let the bread cool down before removing it from the baskets.

Cornbread

 PREPARATION TIME
50 MINUTES

 COOKING TIME
20 MINUTES

 SERVINGS
2 MINI LOAVES

Ingredients:

- 1 cup cornmeal
- 3/4 cup all-purpose flour
- 1 tbsp sugar
- 1 1/2 tsp baking powder
- 1/2 tsp baking soda
- 1/4 tsp salt
- 2 eggs
- 1 1/2 cups buttermilk
- 4 tbsp butter, softened

Instructions:

1. In a bowl, combine the cornmeal, flour, baking powder and salt.
2. In a second bowl, combine the eggs, buttermilk and butter. Combine the wet and dry ingredients.
3. Spray two pans fitted to the two Ninja Foodi 2-Basket Air Fryer baskets and divide the batter between them.
4. Select the BAKE cooking function for Zone 1 and use the TEMP arrows to set the temperature to 182°C (360°F). Use the TIME arrows to set the timer to 25 minutes.
5. Press MATCH COOK and START/PAUSE.
6. After 20 minutes have passed, check if the bread is cooked through. Let the bread down before removing it from the baskets.

BONUS RECIPES
SECTION
FOR
NEW EDITION

Scotch Eggs with air Fryer Parsnips

 PREPARATION TIME
15 MINUTES

 COOKING TIME
15 MINUTES

 SERVINGS
4 PERSONS

Ingredients:

For the Scotch eggs:
- 5 eggs
- 1/2 cup all-purpose flour
- 1 cup breadcrumbs
- 1/4 cup onion, finely minced
- 1 tbsp chives, chopped
- 1 garlic clove, minced
- 1 tsp fresh thyme
- 1/2 tsp paprika
- 350 gr ground pork
- Cooking oil in spray
- Salt and pepper to taste

For the parsnips:
- 4 parsnips.
- Cooking oil in spray
- Salt and pepper to taste

Instructions:

1. In a pot, boil four eggs until hard. Drain, set aside and allow to cool.
2. In a bowl, whisk one egg.
3. In a second bowl, combine the breadcrumbs, onion, chives, garlic, thyme and paprika.
4. Mix the ground pork into the breadcrumb mixture.
5. Coat the hard eggs with the flour, dip them in the whisked egg and cover with the breadcrumb.
6. Spray basket number 1 of the Ninja Foodi 2-Basket Air Fryer with cooking oil and place the coated eggs.
7. Scrub the parsnips, trim the tops and bottoms and cut them into bite-sized pieces.
8. Spray the parsnips with cooking oil and season with salt and pepper to taste.
9. Place the parsnips in basket number 2 in the air fryer.
10. Select the AIR FRY cooking function for Zone 1 and use the TEMP arrows to set the temperature to 180°C.
11. Use the TIME arrows to set the timer to 15 minutes.
12. Program the Zone 2 setting ROAST cooking function, TEMP to 200°C and TIME to 12 minutes.
13. Press SMART FINISH and START/PAUSE.
14. Press PAUSE at the 7-minute mark and flip the eggs and the parsnips. Resume cooking.
15. Serve with your favourite dip and enjoy.

Air Fried Pigs In Blankets with Air Fryer Potato Wedges

 PREPARATION TIME
15 MINUTES

 COOKING TIME
18 MINUTES

 SERVINGS
4 PERSONS

Ingredients:

For the pigs in blankets:
- 1 crescent roll
- 16 smoked sausages
- Cooking oil in spray

For the potato wedges:
- 4 russet potatoes, cut into wedges
- 1/2 tsp paprika
- Salt and pepper to taste
- Cooking oil in spray

Instructions:

1. Place the crescent roll dough on a flat surface and cut it into 16 equal sizes.
2. Roll each sausage with a dough blanket.
3. Spray basket number 1 of the Ninja Foodi 2-Basket Air Fryer with cooking oil and place the rolled sausages.
4. In a mixing bowl, toss the potato wedges with cooking oil and paprika and place them in basket number two.
5. Select the ROAST cooking function for Zone 1 and use the TEMP arrows to set the temperature to 200°C.
6. Use the TIME arrows to set the timer to 15 minutes.
7. Program the Zone 2 setting AIRFRY cooking function, TEMP to 200°C and TIME to 18 minutes.
8. Press SMART FINISH and START/PAUSE.
9. Press PAUSE at the 9-minute mark and flip the sausages and wedges. Resume cooking.
10. Serve with ketchup and enjoy.

Tuna Fishcakes with Air Fryer Jacket Potatoes

PREPARATION TIME
15 MINUTES

COOKING TIME
40 MINUTES

SERVINGS
6 PERSONS

Ingredients:

For the fish cakes:
- 300 gr canned tuna
- 2 eggs
- 1/2 cup breadcrumbs
- 2 tbsp Parmesan cheese
- 1 celery stalk, peeled and minced
- 2 tbsp onion, minced
- 1 garlic clove, minced
- Salt and pepper to taste
- Cooking oil in spray

For the jacket potatoes:
- 4 russet potatoes
- Cooking oil in spray
- Salt and pepper to taste

Instructions:

1. In a mixing bowl, combine the tuna, eggs, breadcrumbs, Parmesan, celery, onion and garlic. Season with salt and pepper.
2. Shape six balls and pat them until flat, around 3/4-inch thick.
3. Place the tuna cakes in basket number 1 of the Ninja Foodi 2-Basket Air Fryer.
4. For the jacket potatoes, prick the potatoes with a fork and rub them with cooking oil. Season with salt and pepper and place in basket number 2.
5. Select the AIR FRY cooking function for Zone 1 and use the TEMP arrows to set the temperature to 180ºC.
6. Use the TIME arrows to set the timer to 12 minutes.
7. Program the Zone 2 setting ROAST cooking function, TEMP to 200ºC and TIME to 40 minutes.
8. Press SMART FINISH and START/PAUSE.
9. Press PAUSE at the 6-minute mark and flip the tuna cakes. Resume cooking.
10. Serve with mayonnaise, a lemon wedge and enjoy.

Air Fryer Fish & Chips

 PREPARATION TIME
15 MINUTES

 COOKING TIME
20 MINUTES

 SERVINGS
2 PERSONS

Ingredients:

For the fish:
- 2 fish fillets
- 1 egg
- 1/2 cup all-purpose flour
- 1/2 tsp paprika
- Salt and pepper to taste

For the chips:
- • 2 cups frozen fries

Instructions:

1. Whisk the egg in a small bowl, and season it with salt, pepper and paprika.
2. Coat the fillets with the egg mixture and cover them with breadcrumbs on all sides.
3. Place the fillets in basket number 1 of the Ninja Foodi 2-Basket Air Fryer.
4. Spray basket number 2 with oil and place the chips.
5. Select the AIR FRY cooking function for Zone 1 and use the TEMP arrows to set the temperature to 200ºC.
6. Use the TIME arrows to set the timer to 10 minutes.
7. Program the Zone 2 setting AIRFRY cooking function, TEMP to 180ºC and TIME to 20 minutes.
8. Press SMART FINISH and START/PAUSE.
9. Press PAUSE at the 5-minute mark and flip the fillets using tongs. Resume cooking.
10. Press PAUSE at the 10-minute mark and shake the chips basket.
11. Serve with tartar sauce and lemon wedges.

Toad In A Hole with Air Fryer Chips

PREPARATION TIME
15 MINUTES

COOKING TIME
20 MINUTES

SERVINGS
4 PERSONS

Ingredients:

For the toad in a hole:
- 2 tbsp butter
- 2 eggs
- 1/2 cup all-purpose flour
- 1/4 white onion, minced
- 1 garlic clove, minced
- 1 tbsp mustard
- Salt and pepper to taste
- 8 sausages

For the chips:
- 1 russet potato
- 1/4 tsp paprika
- Salt and pepper to taste
- Cooking oil in spray

Instructions:

1. Butter four ramekins and set them aside.
2. In a mixing bowl, combine the eggs, flour, onion, garlic, mustard, salt and pepper.
3. Cut the sausages and fold them into the batter.
4. Pour the batter into the ramekins and place them in basket number 1 of the Ninja Foodi 2-Basket Air Fryer.
5. For the chips, use a mandolin to slice the potatoes thinly. Spray them with cooking oil and paprika. Place in basket number 2.
6. Select the ROAST cooking function for Zone 1 and use the TEMP arrows to set the temperature to 180ºC.
7. Use the TIME arrows to set the timer to 20 minutes.
8. Program the Zone 2 setting REHEAT cooking function, TEMP to 200ºC and TIME to 15 minutes.
9. Press SMART FINISH and START/PAUSE.
10. Press PAUSE at the 12-minute mark and shake basket number 2. Resume cooking.
11. Serve with gravy and enjoy!

Bacon Sandwich with Air Fryer Roast Potatoes

 PREPARATION TIME
10 MINUTES

 COOKING TIME
20 MINUTES

 SERVINGS
1 PERSONS

Ingredients:

For the sandwich:
- 2 slices of bread
- 2 slices of Cheddar
- 2 slices of cooked bacon
- 1 tbsp butter

For the roast potatoes:
- 1 cup baby red potatoes
- 1 tsp dried thyme
- Cooking oil in spray
- Salt and pepper to taste

Instructions:

1. Top one slice of bread with cheese and bacon.
2. Spread the butter on the second bread slice. Top the sandwich and press gently.
3. Place the sandwich in basket number 1 of the Ninja Foodi 2-Basket Air Fryer with the crisper plate installed.
4. Prick the baby potatoes with a fork, spray with cooking oil and toss with thyme, salt and pepper. Place in basket number 2.
5. Select the REHEAT cooking function for Zone 1 and use the TEMP arrows to set the temperature to 200°C for 8 minutes.
6. Program the Zone 2 setting ROAST cooking function, TEMP to 200°C and TIME to 20 minutes.
7. Press SMART FINISH and START/PAUSE.
8. Press PAUSE at the 4-minute mark and flip the sandwich. Resume cooking.
9. PAUSE again when 10 minutes remain to shake the potato basket. Resume cooking.
10. Cut the sandwich in half, serve with potatoes and enjoy.

Air Fryer Stuffed Chicken Breasts with Mashed Potato Balls

 PREPARATION TIME
20 MINUTES

 COOKING TIME
20 MINUTES

 SERVINGS
2 PERSONS

Ingredients:

For the chicken:
- 2 chicken breasts, boneless, skinless
- 2 slices of ham
- 2 slices of mozzarella
- 1/2 cup all-purpose flour
- 1/2 tsp dried rosemary
- 1/2 tsp dried thyme
- Salt and pepper to taste
- Cooking oil in spray

For the mashed potato balls:
- 500 gr mashed potatoes
- 1 cup Cheddar, grated
- 1 tbsp chives, chopped
- 1/2 cup all-purpose flour
- 2 eggs
- 1 cup breadcrumbs
- Salt and pepper to taste

Instructions:

1. Using a knife, cut a pocket in each chicken breast and stuff with ham and mozzarella.
2. Combine the flour with the rosemary and thyme. Coat the chicken breasts and place them in basket number 1 of the Ninja Foodi 2-Basket Air Fryer.
3. To make the mashed potato balls, combine the mashed potatoes, cheese and chives in a mixing bowl. Roll into bite-sized balls.
4. Whisk the egg in a small bowl and season with salt and pepper. Coat the balls in egg and cover them with breadcrumbs.
5. Place the mashed potato balls in basket number 2.
6. Select the ROAST cooking function for Zone 1 and use the TEMP arrows to set the temperature to 190ºC.
7. Use the TIME arrows to set the timer to 20 minutes.
8. Program the Zone 2 setting AIR FRY cooking function, TEMP to 200ºC and TIME to 15 minutes.
9. Press SMART FINISH and START/PAUSE.
10. Press PAUSE at the 10-minute mark and flip the chicken using tongs. Shake basket number 2. Resume cooking.
11. Serve with a green salad and your favourite dressing.

Air Fryer Frozen Chicken Nuggets with Air Fryer Carrots

 PREPARATION TIME
5 MINUTES

 COOKING TIME
12 MINUTES

 SERVINGS
2 PERSONS

Ingredients:

For the nuggets:
- 500 grams frozen nuggets
- Cooking oil in spray

For the carrots:
- 2 cups carrots, peeled and cut into sticks.
- 1/2 tsp dried thyme
- Salt and pepper to taste
- Cooking oil in spray

Instructions:

1. Place the crisper plate in basket number 1 in basket number 1 of the Ninja Foodi 2-Basket Air Fryer. Spray with cooking oil and place the chicken nuggets.
2. Spray the carrot sticks and toss them with thyme, salt and pepper. Place in basket number two.
3. Select the AIR FRY cooking function for Zone 1 and use the TEMP arrows to set the temperature to 200ºC.
4. Use the TIME arrows to set the timer to 12 minutes.
5. Press MATCH COOK and START/PAUSE. Both baskets will fry at the same time.
6. Press PAUSE at the 6-minute mark and flip the nuggets. Shake basket number 2. Resume cooking.
7. Serve with ketchup and enjoy!

Air Fryer Tikka Chicken Breast with Roasted Tomatoes

 PREPARATION TIME
15 MINUTES

 COOKING TIME
20 MINUTES

 SERVINGS
2 PERSONS

Ingredients:

For the chicken tikka:
- 2 chicken breasts, boneless, skinless, diced
- 1 green bell pepper, diced
- 1 red bell pepper, diced
- 1/2 onion, sliced
- 2 tbsp tikka seasonings
- Cooking oil in spray

For the roasted tomatoes:
- 4 tomatoes
- Salt and pepper to taste
- Cooking oil in spray

Instructions:

1. Combine the diced chicken with the bell peppers and onion. Spray with cooking oil and toss with tikka seasonings.
2. Install the crisper plate in basket number 1 of the Ninja Foodi 2-Basket Air Fryer and place the chicken.
3. Cut the tomatoes in half, spray with cooking oil and season with salt and pepper. Place in basket number 2.
4. Select the ROAST cooking function for Zone 1 and use the TEMP arrows to set the temperature to 190ºC.
5. Use the TIME arrows to set the timer to 20 minutes.
6. Program the Zone 2 setting ROAST cooking function, TEMP to 200ºC and TIME to 15 minutes.
7. Press SMART FINISH and START/PAUSE.
8. Press PAUSE at the 10-minute mark and flip the chicken using tongs. Resume cooking.
9. Serve and drizzle the tomatoes with olive oil.

Sunday Roast with Air Fryer Cheese Biscuits

PREPARATION TIME
15 MINUTES

COOKING TIME
30 MINUTES

SERVINGS
4 PERSONS

Ingredients:

For the roast:
- 500 grams eye of round roast
- 1 tbsp dried rosemary
- Salt and pepper to taste
- Cooking oil in spray

For the cheese biscuits:
- 1 cup all-purpose flour
- 1 cup Cheddar, shredded
- 1 tbsp butter
- 1 garlic clove
- 1/2 tsp paprika
- 1/2 tsp cayenne pepper
- Salt and pepper to taste
- Cooking oil in spray

Instructions:

1. Spray the roast with cooking oil and rub it with rosemary, salt and pepper. Place in basket number 1 of the Ninja Foodi 2-Basket Air Fryer.
2. In a food processor, add the flour, Cheddar, butter, garlic, paprika, cayenne, salt and pepper. Pulse until a dough forms.
3. Roll the dough into bite-sized pieces and place them in basket number 2.
4. Select the ROAST cooking function for Zone 1 and use the TEMP arrows to set the temperature to 200°C.
5. Use the TIME arrows to set the timer to 30 minutes.
6. Program the Zone 2 setting AIR FRY cooking function, TEMP to 180°C and TIME to 12 minutes.
7. Press SMART FINISH and START/PAUSE.
8. Press PAUSE at the 11-minute mark and turn the roast. Resume cooking.
9. PAUSE again when 6 minutes remain to shake basket number 2. Resume cooking.
10. Check the roast's inner temperature, aiming at 65°C for medium.
11. Serve with gravy and your favourite grilled veggies.

Shepherd's Pie with Air Fryer Apple Chips

PREPARATION TIME
15 MINUTES

COOKING TIME
35 MINUTES

SERVINGS
2 PERSONS

Ingredients:

For the shepherd's pie:
- 250 gr cooked chicken breast, shredded
- 4 tbsp chicken gravy
- 1/4 cup carrots, sliced
- 1/4 cup onions, diced
- 1 cup cooked mashed potatoes
- 1 tbsp butter
- Salt and pepper to taste

For the apple chips:
- 2 apples, sliced
- 1/2 tsp cinnamon
- 1/2 tsp nutmeg
- Cooking oil in spray

Instructions:

1. Butter two ramekins and set aside.
2. In a mixing bowl, combine the chicken breast with the gravy, carrots and onion. Divide the mixture into the ramekins.
3. Top the ramekins with a layer of mashed potatoes and place them in basket number 1 of the Ninja Foodi 2-Basket Air Fryer.
4. Spay the sliced apples and toss with cinnamon and nutmeg. Install the crisper plate in basket number 2 and place the chips.
5. Select the ROAST cooking function for Zone 1 and use the TEMP arrows to set the temperature to 200ºC.
6. Use the TIME arrows to set the timer to 35 minutes.
7. Program the Zone 2 setting AIR FRY cooking function, TEMP to 200ºC and TIME to 18 minutes.
8. Press SMART FINISH and START/PAUSE.
9. Press PAUSE when 9 minutes remain and shake basket number 2. Resume cooking.
10. Drizzle the ramekins with melted butter and serve.

Haggis And Black Pudding Dirty Fries

 PREPARATION TIME
5 MINUTES

 COOKING TIME
20 MINUTES

 SERVINGS
2 PERSONS

Ingredients:

- For the haggis:
- 2 haggis slices
- 2 black pudding slices
- For the dirty fries:
- 2 cup frozen potato fries
- 4 tbsp grated cheddar
- 1 jalapeño pepper, sliced

Instructions:

1. Place the haggis and black pudding slices in basket number 1 of the Ninja Foodi 2-Basket Air Fryer.
2. Install the crisper plate in basket number two and place the fries.
3. Select the ROAST cooking function for Zone 1 and use the TEMP arrows to set the temperature to 200°C.
4. Use the TIME arrows to set the timer to 10 minutes.
5. Program the Zone 2 setting AIR FRY cooking function, TEMP to 180°C and TIME to 20 minutes.
6. Press SMART FINISH and START/PAUSE.
7. Press PAUSE at the 10-minute mark and shake basket number 2. Resume cooking.
8. PAUSE again when 5 minutes remain to flip the haggis and black pudding. Resume cooking.
9. Crumble the haggis and black pudding and toss with the fries along with the cheese. Allow to melt.
10. Garnish with jalapeño slices.

Yorkshire Pudding with Air Fryer Stuffing Balls

 PREPARATION TIME
25 MINUTES

 COOKING TIME
18 MINUTES

 SERVINGS
4 PERSONS

Ingredients:

For the pudding:
- 1 egg
- 4 tbsp flour
- 1/4 cup milk
- 1/4 cup water
- 1/2 tsp salt
- 1 tbsp butter

For the stuffing balls:
- 1 tbsp butter, softened
- 1/4 cup onion, minced
- 1/4 cup celery, chopped
- 2 cups breadcrumbs
- 1 egg
- Salt and pepper to taste
- Cooking oil in spray

Instructions:

1. Butter four ramekins and set aside.
2. In a mixing bowl, combine the egg, flour, milk, water and salt to form a batter.
3. Pour the batter into the ramekins and place them in basket number 1 of the Ninja Foodi 2-Basket Air Fryer.
4. For the stuffing balls, combine the butter, onion, celery, breadcrumbs, egg, salt and butter in a food processor to form a dough.
5. Roll the dough into bite-sized balls and refrigerate for 15 minutes.
6. Place the balls in basket number 2.
7. Select the ROAST cooking function for Zone 1 and use the TEMP arrows to set the temperature to 200°C.
8. Use the TIME arrows to set the timer to 18 minutes.
9. Program the Zone 2 setting AIR-FRY cooking function, TEMP to 180°C and TIME to 10 minutes.
10. Press SMART FINISH and START/PAUSE.
11. Press PAUSE when 5 minutes remain and shake basket number 2. Resume cooking.
12. Serve and enjoy.

Meat Pie with Air Fryer Hash Browns

 PREPARATION TIME
30 MINUTES

 COOKING TIME
18 MINUTES

 SERVINGS
2 PERSONS

Ingredients:

For the meat pies:
- 250 gr ground beef
- 1 medium potato, in cubes
- 1 garlic clove, minced
- 1/4 white onion, minced
- 1/2 tsp paprika
- Salt and pepper to taste
- 200 gr puff pastry dough
- Cooking oil

For the hash browns:
- 2 russet potatoes
- 2 tbsp breadcrumbs
- 1/2 tsp garlic powder
- 1/2 tsp onion powder
- Salt and pepper to taste

Instructions:

1. In a frying pan, add a splash of cooking oil and sauté the onion and garlic until caramelised and fragrant.
2. Add the potatoes and cook for 5 more minutes.
3. Add the ground beef and incorporate. Cook until brown.
4. Season with paprika, salt and pepper.
5. Roll the puff pastry and cut into two 10 cm circles.
6. Fill each circle with the seasoned meat and fold. Seal by pinching with your fingers.
7. Spray the meat pies with oil and place them in basket number 1 of the Ninja Foodi 2-Basket Air Fryer.
8. To make the hash browns, grate the potatoes and soak in cold water for 10 minutes. Rinse and pat dry.
9. Combine the potato with the breadcrumbs, and season with garlic powder, onion powder, salt and pepper.
10. Shape the hash browns with your hands.
11. Install the crisper plate in basket number 2 and spray with cooking oil. Place the hash browns.
12. Select the ROAST cooking function for Zone 1 and use the TEMP arrows to set the temperature to 180°C.
13. Use the TIME arrows to set the timer to 18 minutes.
14. Press MATCH COOK and START/PAUSE. Both baskets will fry at the same time.
15. Serve and enjoy!

Steak And Ale Pie with Air Fryer Garlic Bread

 PREPARATION TIME
25 MINUTES

 COOKING TIME
12 MINUTES

 SERVINGS
2 PERSONS

Ingredients:

For the pie:
- Shortcut pastry
- 500 gr ground beef
- 1 can ale beer
- 1/2 white onion, diced
- 1 garlic clove, minced
- 2 tbsp tomato puree
- 1 tbsp corn starch
- Salt and pepper to taste
- Cooking oil

For the garlic bread:
- 4 slices of bread
- 4 tsp softened butter
- 1 tbsp garlic powder
- Salt and pepper to taste

Instructions:

1. Add oil to a frying pan and sauté the onion and garlic.
2. Cook the ground beef until brown and the tomato puree, corn starch, salt and pepper.
3. Add the ale and stir until reduced.
4. Roll the shortcut pastry and cut it into circles to cover the bottom and sides of 2 ramekins.
5. Place the pastry in the ramekins and fill it with the meat mixture. Place in basket number 1 of the Ninja Foodi 2-Basket Air Fryer.
6. Spread the butter on the bread. Season with garlic powder, salt and pepper.
7. Place the bread in basket number 2.
8. Select the ROAST cooking function for Zone 1 and use the TEMP arrows to set the temperature to 200ºC (390ºF).
9. Use the TIME arrows to set the timer to 12 minutes.
10. Program the Zone 2 setting REHEAT cooking function, TEMP to 180ºC and TIME to 10 minutes.
11. Press SMART FINISH and START/PAUSE.
12. Serve and enjoy.

Black Pudding with Air Fryer Grilled Cheese

 PREPARATION TIME
10 MINUTES

 COOKING TIME
10 MINUTES

 SERVINGS
2 PERSONS

Ingredients:

- For the black pudding:
- 4 Black pudding slices
- For the grilled cheese:
- 4 sourdough bread slices
- 2 tbsp butter, softened
- 2 Cheddar slices

Instructions:

1. Place the black pudding slices in basket number 1 of the Ninja Foodi 2-Basket Air Fryer.
2. Spread the butter on the bread slices, top with cheese and top the sandwiches. Place them in basket number 2.
3. Select the ROAST cooking function for Zone 1 and use the TEMP arrows to set the temperature to 180°C.
4. Use the TIME arrows to set the timer to 7 minutes.
5. Program the Zone 2 setting REHEAT cooking function, TEMP to 180°C (360°F) and TIME to 10 minutes.
6. Press SMART FINISH and START/PAUSE.
7. Press PAUSE at the 5-minute mark and flip the grilled cheese. Resume cooking.
8. Serve and enjoy!

Air-Fried Mars Bars

 PREPARATION TIME
20 MINUTES

 COOKING TIME
8 MINUTES

 SERVINGS
4 PERSONS

Ingredients:

- 1 cup all-purpose flour
- 1/3 cup butter, softened
- 3 tbsp granulated sugar
- 4 Mars Bars
- Icing sugar as a garnish
- Cooking oil in spray

Instructions:

1. In a mixing bowl, combine the flour, butter and sugar. Add water if needed until you get a dough.
2. Roll the dough on a floured surface, cut it into 4 squares and roll the mars bars with it.
3. Place two Mars bars on basket no.1 and two in basket number 2.
4. Select the AIR FRY cooking function for Zone 1 and use the TEMP arrows to set the temperature to 180ºC.
5. Use the TIME arrows to set the timer to 8 minutes.
6. Press MATCH COOK and START/PAUSE. Both baskets will fry at the same time.
7. Press PAUSE at the 4-minute mark and flip the bars. Resume cooking.
8. Serve and dust with icing sugar.

Air Fryer Apple And Blackberry Crumble

 PREPARATION TIME
10 MINUTES

 COOKING TIME
10 MINUTES

 SERVINGS
4 PERSONS

Ingredients:

- 2 tsp butter
- 1 cup of diced apples
- 1 cup of blackberries
- 1 tbsp granulated sugar
- 1 tsp cinnamon
- 4 tbsp rolled oats
- 4 tbsp all-purpose flour
- 4 tbsp brown sugar
- 1/2 tsp salt
- 4 tbsp water
- Whipped cream as a garnish

Instructions:

1. In a mixing bowl, combine all the ingredients except for the whipped cream and mix well.
2. Transfer the mixture into four ramekins, cover them with aluminium foil and place them in both baskets.
3. Select the ROAST cooking function for Zone 1 and use the TEMP arrows to set the temperature to 180ºC.
4. Use the TIME arrows to set the timer to 10 minutes.
5. Press MATCH COOK and START/PAUSE. Both baskets will fry at the same time.
6. Press PAUSE at the 5-minute mark and remove the foil. Resume cooking.
7. Garnish with whipped cream and serve.

Giant Chocolate Chip Cookies

PREPARATION TIME
15 MINUTES

COOKING TIME
10 MINUTES

SERVINGS
2 PERSONS

Ingredients:

- 4 tbsp melted butter
- 4 tbsp brown sugar
- 2 tbsp granulated sugar
- 2 egg yolks
- 1 tsp vanilla
- 1 cup flour
- 1/2 tsp baking powder
- 1/2 tsp salt
- 1/2 cup chocolate chips

Instructions:

1. In a mixing bowl, combine the butter with the brown sugar and the granulated sugar. Add the yolks, vanilla.
2. Add the flour while stirring. Once incorporated, add the baking powder and salt.
3. Fold in the chocolate chips and divide the batter in two.
4. Line the baskets of the Ninja Foodi 2-Basket Air Fryer with parchment paper and pour the batter into both.
5. Select the ROAST cooking function for Zone 1 and use the TEMP arrows to set the temperature to 200°C.
6. Use the TIME arrows to set the timer to 10 minutes.
7. Press MATCH COOK and START/PAUSE. Both baskets will fry at the same time.
8. Allow the cookies to cool before removing them. Enjoy!

Air Fryer Scones

 PREPARATION TIME
15 MINUTES

 COOKING TIME
12 MINUTES

 SERVINGS
6 PERSONS

Ingredients:

- 450 gr self-rising flour
- 80 gr butter, in cubes
- 1 cup of milk
- 1/2 tsp salt

Instructions:

1. Combine the ingredients in a food processor until a smooth dough forms.
2. Shape six bite-sized balls.
3. Place the crisper platters into the Ninja Foodi 2-Basket Air Fryer baskets and place the dough balls.
4. Select the ROAST cooking function for Zone 1 and use the TEMP arrows to set the temperature to 200ºC.
5. Use the TIME arrows to set the timer to 12 minutes.
6. Press MATCH COOK and START/PAUSE. Both baskets will begin to fry at the same time.
7. Serve with cream and jam!

CONCLUSION

You have completed your first step to culinary freedom. You can now cook in an unheated kitchen.

The next step from here is to explore even further and find your own culinary footing! Learn the basics from this recipes, and come up with your very own awesome Ninja Foodi Friendly recipes and make your ultimate meal plan!

The Ninja Foodi possesses the unique ability to micro-wave food, so if you are looking for a one-stop-shop for your food-cooking needs, it really doesn't get any better than the Ninja Foodi! You see, with just one appliance, you will be able to make the staples of your diet! You will be able to make rice, soup, stews, pastas, deep fried foods, and vegetable dishes, all with the simple touch of a button! So, what you are telling yourself at. This is far too good to be true! I know, I know! Of course, the question on your mind would definitely be: how can the Ninja Foodi deliver such great attributes for such a low price? Instead of having to spend over a hundred dollars on a rice cooker, a slow cooker, and an air fryer, the Ninja Foodi has all of those functions in one tiny, inexpensive appliance. Not only does it have those attributes, but it is able to take your cooking to the next level. Now, you can make the most delicious steamed or deep fried foods in your own home! Your whole family will be motivated to eat clean and more often, all because you singlehandedly took control of your kitchen! Lastly, if you feel like your Ninja Foodi is just not up to snuff, don't worry! Ninja Foodi is not like any other appliance that you will probably ever encounter. A Ninja Foodist always trusts and follows their instincts, and you should too. The Ninja Foodist rewards us for doing so. Ninja Foodist that is what we ninja's are training to become. If you look at the Ninja Foodi Cam you'll notice that it is almost the same size as the Ninja Foodi itself, but for ninja training purposes we must use the Cam to train our reflexes. Just like one must when learning to use a silent but deadly weapon like the Shurikon. A Ninja Foodist learns to be able to respond to any situation in a relatively quick manner, and when training like this, we must do so much faster than ever before. Like Ninja Foodist's already do, we must do so while dealing with a situation on a much larger scale.

Fire is still a big deal, so keep on practicing … please. Try to avoid meat or fish in most of your meals, or you'll get massive heartburn. Enjoy your Ninja Cooking skills! It is fun to create new recipes and experiment. You don't need a microwave, just add foil, aluminum foil, etc to your dishes to be heated. Making beans in your Ninja Cooking is great. Since they are very water soluble, they will add their own water to your dish when you cook them. Plates, bowls, baking sheets and glass will work just as well as induction cooktops or a non-microwave oven.

You are now a culinary ninja. Enjoy cooking your favorite Ninja Foodi Friendly meals and recipes!

INDEX

Hope You Enjoyed The Recipes

If you liked the recipes leave a review on amazon and let others know about it, so they can enjoy the good foods at their home easily

Sharing is caring

Don't forget to share the recipes with your friends and family

THANK YOU